GROW A PAIR

Harnessing authentic masculine power to restore
love and balance to your life and relationships

Greg Paul

www.thesovereignsway.com

ISBN-10: 1544224001
ISBN-13: 978-1544224008

DEDICATION

This book I dedicate to the goddess rising, and to the most astonishing goddess I have ever met – whose remarkable wisdom, true divine feminine nature and the breathtakingly deep connection we share have made this book possible. You know who you are.

CONTENTS

PREFACE

Sisters – this book is written as much for you as it is we men. Whilst the motivation for it is the genuine hope that it may serve in some small way to nurture us men into the fullness of our authentic masculine potential, I hope you read it too. We need your love, compassion and understanding if we are to do this, and it is my deepest wish that you may find in these pages such an understanding. The divide between the sexes is huge and really only just coming to mass awareness. This divide exists on both sides and we need to close it together. In fact only together can we truly heal it all. Much of this book is dedicated to how we can work together to achieve that goal.

Brothers – writing this book has been a truly alchemical process. Though I would never have admitted this before, it is, in truth, the first time I have ever published something publically that truly comes from the depths of my heart – alchemizing the terrifying reality of the depth of suffering that I and the male collective have inflicted on the sacred feminine, and in the face of the abject shock which it instilled, has been interesting to say the least. But the results were magnificent – this book is just one of the remarkable outcomes, and I am honored to share it with you.

A word of advice – take this book slowly. There's a lot of information packed tightly in these 140 or so pages. It's designed as a handbook that you can keep returning to as you advance your own condition. Though your manly control tendencies my like to try, there's really no need to understand everything in one go!

INTRODUCTION

The male dominance paradigm and the false-light scourge of inverted male power is threatening our very existence as a species. Men must find a new way to exist, and not just to exist but thrive.

Love has been lost. To most of us it is not even a memory. Most of us, both men and women, have never experienced real pure love at any point in our lives. And we are aching for it. Our souls are crying out in pain at the loss of love and the pain of an endless longing that is never fulfilled. Nothing will change so long as we remain in denial of the true depth of that loss and the degree of our continuing participation in the inverted male power game which prevents any kind of resolution. For it is our participation in it that is the self-generated power-source which perpetuates our own endless suffering.

Just look at some of the symptoms playing out in the world today. Children are taken from families and trafficked to pedophile rings to satiate the sexual desires of emotionally injured men. Women are practically and emotionally overpowered, their best efforts to address this with the feminist movement only serving to turn most women into inverted male power-wielding men themselves. In almost every home throughout the land, children have their innocence robbed on a daily basis – blaming, shaming, abusing, over-nurturing – by our own hands. It is a male dominant culture, and the women raise the men to perpetuate it! We have all lost our way. And it's all driven by our personal emotional wounding and the unseen & unspoken divide between the sexes – that pain of separation between the masculine and feminine which we all sense but are too afraid to even admit the terrifying pain of to ourselves.

Life is meant to be loving… all of it. But we have been given the gift of free-will, so we've always had the ability to manifest whatever reality we choose. We just used it to choose this reality over one of ever-increasing love and potential.

It's not difficult to explain why we are where we are and why it is so difficult to break the cycle. The whole game is anchored as a multi-generational disease – 'born into sin' – and cemented by familial relationships.

Every boy learns what treatment he can expect from a woman from his mother. He will expect the same treatment from all the women in his life. Whether it be that they are responsible to meet his unhealthy emotional needs, or that they are controlling, short-tempered and abusive. And he will draw that to him in the future because he is a match to it.

And he learns how to treat a woman from his father – how to communicate and relate emotionally – and he will usually believe whatever that behavior is to be appropriate and right. He will also learn from his father how to accept, expect from or make demands of, a woman who meets his unhealthy emotional needs, or how to accept, fight against, submit to or domineer, in response to more aggressive behavior.

Every girl learns what treatment she can expect from a man from her father. She will expect the same treatment from all the men in her life. Whether it be that she is responsible to meet all their unhealthy emotional needs, or that they are controlling, short-tempered, abusive or distant.

And she learns how to treat a man from her mother – how to communicate and relate emotionally. And she will usually believe whatever that behavior is to be appropriate and right. She will also learn from her mother how to validate, or resist, his emotionally addictive behaviors.

So most all boys are taught to maintain the male dominance paradigm, and most all girls are taught how to encourage them.

One feels shame, the other anger. And even if we have been strong enough to not repeat our familial dynamics with our own children, if we haven't healed our trauma that resulted from those events, all we ever do is push back in the opposite direction and create the opposite (i.e. same) problem.

We all feel powerless to change it. But we are not powerless to change it. *We* created everything we see here, because *we* didn't understand natural law. *We* did it… all of it.

All we need to do to break this dystopian cycle is to understand the truth of the natural loving laws of the universe and apply them in our lives. In particular those that relate to personal healing, the realization of one's true human potential, and mastering the use of our free-will. Until now, these laws have not really been presented in a singular coherent presentation. That's what this book is all about.

These laws require us, if we are to discover our authentic masculine potential and heal the divide between the masculine and feminine, to first of all accept the degree to which we are actually perpetrating our false-light bullshit in the world; they require us to face the aspects of ourselves that we have hitherto hidden from; they require us to address our entitlement issues; they require us to face our own darkness and be willing to feel, everything, fully; they require us to develop our innate capacity to nurture; they require us to stop deflecting the tremendous amount of shame we subconsciously carry, and feel it instead; they require us to repent, meaning to fully acknowledge our actions and feel the accompanying emotions, for each and every act of energetic rape we have committed, likewise to forgive each and every act perpetrated against us; and, to paraphrase a rather brilliant article I once read – they require each of us as men to "look our distrust of the feminine squarely in the eyes and tell it to fuck off."

If we're going to do this, we need to dream together a new dream – we need to envision a loving reality.

A loving reality would be one which is in balance with itself. First and foremost there would be balance between masculine and feminine; they would be working in harmony with each other, in love, to co-create the loving reality that natural law itself would create were free-will not part of the equation. Secondly, and as a direct result of masculine/feminine balance, every child would be raised with little or no emotional injury, and with the knowledge of how to immediately heal any injuries that did unexpectedly occur. They would receive love unconditionally, in the presence of masculine/feminine harmony, and perpetuate this new meme with their own future partners and children.

In a loving reality, everyone would be masters of the art of the true man-woman relationship, and everyone would know that the first requirement of such a beauty is for both parties to be in love with themselves; for both parties to have made themselves their own primary relationship partner; for each to be their own reason for being.

Imagine for a moment how such a relationship would *feel*... envision your future with me.

There is complete and total freedom – you need nothing from each other, and consequently you give and receive *everything* you have ever dreamed of – with pure love.

You are each other's greatest teacher. You respect her wisdom and everything about her and she shares herself with you... all of herself. She respects your wisdom and everything about you and you share yourself with her too... all of yourself. As you nurture each other she blossoms further and further into her own goddess embodiment, and you into ever greater heights of your own sovereign potential. An exponentially expansive spiral to ecstasy is the train you ride each moment together.

No one is having 'control' because you are in a complete union state, acting as one. You have complete individuality in terms of your thoughts and actions, but you are in full telepathic communication – you know *everything* about each other, your physical energy centers spin in time, and your physical hearts beat as one. You are both in full alignment with natural law, so you always perceive the right choice to be the same.

The sex is mind-blowing – you travel to the stars, or wherever you choose, but this is nothing compared to the state of energetic love making with which you're both engaged – twenty-four-seven – that has you feeling what each other feels and sharing sexual energy in a divine flow of co-creative potentiality. As a result your shared capacity to manifest breathtaking co-creations is *far* in advance of anything you could ever achieve as individuals… even as a fully self-realized man and woman. Your environments reflect the inner perfection and excellence that you each and together are.

Wouldn't this be preferable to your current relationship with the feminine?

Likewise, in a loving reality, every child would know that they are loved and have no need to box away pieces of their own soul in order to survive, and every child would grow up knowing only the loving way to engage relationship with the opposite sex; being naturally capable of, and effectively guaranteed to, create the same, or better for themselves.

Imagine for a moment how such a child would experience life; how your own life would have been if you had experienced this yourself:

Your mother has no fear, anxiety, grief or terror lurking in the back ground; no negative thoughts or co-dependencies influencing her state of being or creating emotional pain, so from the moment you are conceived to the moment you are born, you experience only loving, supportive emotions. By the time you are born you are already loved fully. Your birth experience is orgasmic for both you and her.

She and your father love you completely – a pure divine love that permeates every cell of your being. You experience their unfaltering

11

perfect states of nurturance and protection. You grow up experiencing your mother as a goddess and your father as a god and there never comes a time where you are disappointed that they are not – because they are, and so are you, because it is all you know.

You never develop any concept of being left wanting for anything, because they fulfill your every true need without thought or sense of obligation. Nor do they ever limit your individuality because they always serve you with true unconditional love and always put your true needs above their own emotional needs – they have no demands of you… ever.

Your education is an education in love, beginning with the natural laws of the universe, so you will never inadvertently harm yourself or others for want of knowledge – you know everything, because you have never been forced to close yourself off from the truth. Everything you have ever seen or heard is in perfect alignment with absolute truth, so you have never learnt to doubt or question yourself.

You express your emotions freely, you are never suppressed; never attacked, shamed or diminished, so your innocence remains completely intact. You marvel at the stories of how the world used to be, wondering what shame, guilt, grief, or terror ever felt like.

What life would you now be leading if you had experienced such a childhood?

This book is about us charting the realistic course to making this new dream a living reality in both our lives and the greater world, for the benefit of ourselves and our children. It is a dream which, if we could see the truth for ourselves, is but a hairs breadth from being realized for each of us. We simply need to make the choice for it to be so.

What makes me an authority on this subject, you may be asking…

Well not much actually. I was simply fortunate enough that a true goddess walked into my life one day who drew out all the remaining false-light bullshit in me like poison from a wound – a woman who stood toe-to-toe with me, never flinching, as we triggered in each other the deepest darkest wounds within and faced it together; staring each other down as we personified each other's terror. And then other women came in to the mix – a match to this 'relationship beyond definition' frequency and we worked through more stuff still. And then I formed a training school – The Sovereign's Way Academy – where others could heal themselves, and more, in the nurturing embrace of conscious community.

I had been on this trajectory for a while though by the time all this occurred – an awakening to love some 12 years earlier began a voyage of self-discovery that continues to this day. During these years I also co-founded multiple organizations that sought to return love, truth and balance to the human experience – most notably the New Earth Project/Nation and the International Tribunal for Natural Justice – but it was only really ever the goddesses in my life that made this book possible. That and eight years of dedicated inquiry into the nature of the natural loving laws of the universe and a whole load of trial and error application!

The benefits for us as men of transmuting the inverted power dynamics within us and stepping into our true authentic masculine potential, are incalculable. Love, happiness, wealth, success, are things most of us continue to strive for, and yet the truth is that true love, real happiness, guilt-free wealth and the kind of success we really crave, are only possible when we step truly into our authentic masculine power and authority. If you are still, at least in part, selfishly motivated, that's ok… try to look to that which this book is calling you toward as the ultimate, and only, solution to those aspects of non-fulfillment you may still experience – it really is to all our benefit. Really though, the ultimate gift which we receive when we find the courage to be fully transparent and truthful with ourselves, and engage this most sacred of journeys, is the gift of true divine love relationships with real goddesses, which really does make it all worthwhile! It's really that simple – owning the truth of you equals love… in every way.

There are many paths to enlightened self-mastery, and I am not suggesting that any one is better than another; however the journey from A to the imaginary Z can be taken in as much of a straight line or windy path as we choose. The one thing that every path has in common, whether they ever speak of it or not, is that they all lead to the condition of being in alignment with universal natural law.

By the time you have finished this book you will have a comprehensive understanding of natural law as it relates to personal evolution – you will at last have knowledge of the rules of the game of life that have thus far eluded you. You will learn how to apply the natural loving laws of the universe most efficiently in pursuit of your own self-mastery, and you will learn how to develop the qualities which will help you apply those laws most effectively in your life.

You'll also discover how the road to hell is literally paved with good intentions – how the inverted male power game is unwittingly seeded in the heart of most every young male child, the various ways in which those seeds are watered by family and society and how most every well intentioned effort to break this diabolical scenario by grown men only serves to fortify it further. We also look at the more subtle movements of this power game to show just how deep it really runs so you can see more clearly how your own imbalanced dynamics are structured and thus where to apply the natural laws in your own life to best advantage.

If you can truly on-board and apply this knowledge to engage the process that this book calls you toward, then that new dream we have envisioned *will* become your living reality.

The choice we are all faced with is to realign with natural law, grow in love and be reborn each day, or ignore the law, decline in love and die a slow death each day. The latter choice can only have two outcomes – a much harder healing process when we do finally decide to align with the loving laws of the universe, or eternal suffering and degradation. The only question we ought to ask ourselves is what do I choose for my soul?

There is really only one quality that determines whether a man is truly a man or not – his willingness, or unwillingness, to face his own shit and embrace all of who he really is – to feel his grief, feel his shame, repent for his cuntishness and thereby become love.

This may sound difficult, but personal growth is not as hard as it seems, we just like to make it that way. Growth is *not* a process – most every occurrence of growth we experience happens in an instant. It seems like a process because we spend inordinate amounts of time establishing the right circumstances or environment in which growth can occur. The process is creating the environment. The growth is instantaneous. What if we knew, relative to each instance of growth we were seeking, what the right environment was for that growth to occur? Our growth would be instantaneous.

The purpose of this book is to articulate those environments which relate to the transcendence of inverted male power, so you can create those environments for yourself and more easily experience instantaneous growth or in this case, more specifically, instantaneous healing, growth and embodiment of true self-mastered masculine authority.

I don't want you to believe anything you see written here – I want you to experience and know it for yourself.... all of it, in its inherent beauty and perfection. If we follow the path laid out for us by universal natural law in this regard, there is no vision of future perfection that is beyond our reach... *none.*

Brothers, it's time to wake from our slumber... our time has come.

1 A FALSE-LIGHT SCOURGE

The false-light scourge of inverted male power is responsible for *all* the dysfunction we see when we look out at the world – all the sadness, all the suffering, all the brutalization of innocence.

Inverted male power is, to sum it up in a word, rape – rape of innocence in the first instance, and rape for the sake of it after that. And that is really not too harsh a word – inverted male power (whether exercised by a man or a woman) is the theft of the life essence of another; taking without permission. It is no less damaging to the soul condition of either the victim or the perpetrator than physical rape, and we do it every day… almost all of us, in some subtle way, to almost everyone we encounter.

The point of this book is to end this dystopian meme once and for all.

This is not me I hear you say – I don't do that! I said that too – especially after clearing a lot of my shit out some years back, there was no way I was going to accept that there was a whole load more… but there was. In this book I'll share some personal stories to show you just how much more. But suffice it to say for now that since seeing and transmuting this in myself, I can say in all honesty that, even given the circles which my work has had me walk in for many years and the thousands of conscious men I have met as a result, I have only ever met in the flesh *one* man who has verifiably cleaned himself of *all* expressions of inverted male power … *one*.

The depth of suffering which the female collective has inflicted on the sacred masculine is equally shocking of course, but that's not what this book is about! Nor will it ever be our consideration if we are serious about truly embracing our authentic masculine power.

How is it that any of us look out at the world and continue to live as we do? The answer is simple – denial. There is a huge disconnect between what we see when we look out at the world, and the fact that we are the ones responsible for what we see. We don't believe that *we* are actually doing it – it's everyone else, and yet in truth it is not, it is *you*. The proof of this denial is that your life is not already a reflection of perfect joy, beauty and love – which is the inherent condition of all who are in harmony with true law and not busy killing love. We might understand this intellectually, but we don't believe it really.

The truth of who and what you are in this moment likely involves an awful lot of suppressed pain, false beliefs, co-dependency and narcissistic traits which collectively express themselves through you as what I have come to call inverted male power.

In a very real sense, this journey to embodying authentic masculine power is one of acceptance – acceptance of what is; acceptance of our own darkness; acceptance of what was done to us as children; acceptance of our shame for what we have done; acceptance of our abandonment by the feminine… acceptance that we are full of shit.

For me, to go through this process has been amazing. To transmute pain into a blazing inferno of love; to have the feeling of finally coming back online; to feel human and fully alive – transcendent and yet grounded – for the first time; to be able to open to previously unimaginable depths of intimacy with others; to reconstitute the entire source-code of my life to one of love, harmony and grace. Wow – what a gift.

This is the crucible…

2 UNIVERSAL NATURAL LAW

Before we delve any deeper into deconstructing the male dominance paradigm, let's take a look at universal natural law – natural law for short from here on in (or natural loving laws of the universe when I'm feeling exuberant!).

Try to bear these laws in mind as you read through the rest of the book – make it a habit to dissect how situations are out of alignment with the laws, not just in this book, but in your reality in general. As you do this, you will become increasingly perceptive of the true difference between right and wrong. Understanding right and wrong in the context of natural law is actually *very* simple – it is a wrong to cause harm to a living being, including yourself. Everything else is a natural right. The biggest problem we have is that, because of our emotional wounding and the corresponding false belief structures and coping mechanisms we created to hide from the pain we have endured, we don't actually have a very clear idea of what actually constitutes harm, and we therefore exercise our perceived 'rights' at the cost of others. By the end of this book, what actually constitutes harm should be much clearer!

Natural law is the framework that governs the use and operation of consciousness within the multi-dimensional Universe. It provides a set of immutable principles that govern the behavior of life in general and, in the case of human beings having free will, the consequences of that behavior. Natural law offers us the keys to transcending the inverted male power game, stepping into true self-mastery, and otherwise architecting a simpler more creative life in general. We're not going to look at all the natural laws here, that would be impossible, only those that relate to personal healing, the realization of one's true human potential, and mastering the use of our free-will.

When you look at these laws, try to really comprehend them. Can you see how remarkably perfect they are? What a gift they are? Now that you know them... If you can comprehend them deeply enough, and you actually allow them to govern your actions going forward, it will change your life forever.

All we need to do to end this male dominance paradigm once and for all is to understand and apply these laws. If you take away only one thing from this book, please make that one thing an understanding of, and desire to apply, these laws.

The Law of Attraction

Like attracts like. For the purpose of this discussion, the Law of Attraction exists to draw experiences to you so that you can see more clearly where you are actually at on your own path of self-discovery – they are *your* natural attractions, based on *who* you are. They will change when you change, and the Law of Attraction is simply trying to show you where you are now and what things you need to work with in order that your natural state will improve. When you do this you will witness an improvement in your attractions. The Law of Attraction is the gift of insight we have been given to light the path.

Despite mountains of confusing literature to the contrary, one cannot get better attractions through want or desire without addressing the cause of the previously faulty wants or desires – whilst you may employ the Law of Mentality, which we cover shortly, to 'attract' things into your life, you may only do so to the degree to which you are *already* an energetic match to the attraction sought because 1. The Law of Attraction does *not* attract what you want; it attracts what you are, and 2. You cannot falsify yourself in order to get better attractions. The only way to have consistently better experiences in your life, and not add to the problem we're seeking to address with the real work, is to do the real work. When we try to use any natural law in a way it was not intended or designed to be used, we are operating out of harmony with that law, which will only bring a decline in our condition not the improvement sought.

To maximize the potential of this law on our path of healing, and life in general, we respond to every event (attraction) in our lives by first looking at what the attraction is trying to show us about ourselves, *before* we take any action in response to the event. Perhaps you lost your job? The appropriate way to respond to this event in the context of the Law of Attraction is to use the processes described later in this book to understand *what* your soul may be trying to tell you about your life. Perhaps your soul is reflecting to you that it is no longer part of your plan to be divesting sovereignty to third party employers; that it is time for you to follow your passion? Consider – what are your options right now... more specifically, what is the third option that you've not yet seen?

The Law of Cause & Effect

Every cause has an effect and every effect has a cause. For the purpose of this discussion, the Law of Cause & Effect points to a drastic shift we must undergo if we are to effect meaningful change in our lives and the world in which we live. The fear-based heart of our inverted male power dynamics causes us to act reactively in the world. When an attraction occurs in our life that is unwanted – an effect – we immediately react to the effect, and any action we take in response is invariably seeking to mitigate the consequences of that effect. Whilst it is not inappropriate to act to mitigate the consequences of an effect, doing so does nothing to address the *cause* of that effect. Inevitably the effect will continue to play out in our lives as other attractions bear the same experience. If we are to stop attracting the effect, we must address the cause.

To maximize the potential of this law on our path of healing, and life in general, we use our feelings to ascertain what the causes of our attractions are, and engage the Laws of Repentance and Forgiveness to remove them. Continuing with the losing your job example, the appropriate way to respond to this event in the context of the Law of Cause and Effect is to use the tools shared later in this book to discover what the emotional cause of the attraction is *before* seeking out new employment. Perhaps, for example, you are harboring some very specific false beliefs about love which generate a lack of self-worth that is causing you to attract events that consolidate the lack (that you will need to clear before a brighter future is possible in either new employment or your own passion-based enterprise)?

The Law of Polarity

Everything is created dual in the Universe. Opposites are the same in nature, they only differ in degree. Hence why the Law of Attraction will usually attract opposites, especially in relationships between two beings of free-will. It is the Law of Polarity which is ultimately responsible for the 'mirror' effect in relationship.

To maximize the potential of this law on our path of healing, and life in general, we must bring balance to each of the opposites in our experience – masculine/feminine, right hemisphere of brain/left hemisphere of brain, desire for freedom/need for security, etc. We balance these opposites by embracing both within us and alchemizing them in the cauldron which is our activated human heart... more on that in Chapter 9.

The relationship attractions we receive once we have done this will have the permanent effect of being 'complementary,' i.e. where the individual strengths of our balanced selves complement each other, rather than the temporary and subsequently troublesome effect of 'completion,' i.e. where our imbalanced, co-dependent natures look to the other to complete our otherwise incomplete feeling-state.

The Law of Vibration

Everything is energy and everything is in motion. Therefore everything is energy in motion – e-motion. Motion of energy occurs through vibration. The higher the frequency of one's vibration, the greater one's natural alignment with the other laws. Of all emotion, love carries the highest frequency. Love is the only emotion which characterizes a true alignment with natural law. When one masters love, one masters law, and one master's life.

To maximize the potential of this law on our path of healing, and life in general, we simply need to make our sole purpose in life to grow in love. Doing this is a case of cultivating all of the basic qualities which are the prerequisites to a loving life – self-love, commitment to truth, faith and a willingness to feel. We cover the development of these qualities fully in Chapter 8.

The Law of Mentality

Everything in the universe is forged of consciousness. Consciousness is activated by mind – all creation begins with thought. The quality of thought of a being having free-will dictates the quality of the experience of that being.

We take responsibility for what we create by being responsible for what we think. Since most of us are not in conscious control of what we think, we need to first become so. This will happen as a natural bi-product of deconstructing our false selves, which is what this book is all about.

To maximize the potential of this law on our path of healing, and life in general, we simply need to channel our mental capacities toward life-affirming creative pursuits and cease employing them in a manner which is obstructive of this deconstruction process.

The Law of Forgiveness & Repentance

Where there has been a transgression of natural law either by or against a being having free-will, the soul condition of that being is worsened. The Law of Forgiveness & Repentance is the remedy which is offered to both the transgressor and the victim to heal the damage caused. Repentance is the aspect of the law which exists as a remedy to those who have caused harm. Forgiveness is the aspect of the law which exists as a remedy to those who have received harm. Both require the release of all suppressed emotion which exists as a result of the transgression – that's what forgiveness and repentance really is.

Repentance is achieved when one has truly accepted, and felt the corresponding emotions of, the harm they have caused, and have redressed as far as possible the physical ramifications of the action.

Repentance is difficult to describe – it cannot be conceptualized, it can only be felt. The feeling state of repentance is not one of guilt or shame, though one will almost certainly pass through one or both of those, rather it is a *knowing* of right and wrong to such an extent that one will never be able to commit the same act ever again. You could say that repentance is the act of releasing the emotions that cause you to express inverted male power.

Forgiveness on the other hand is very easy to describe, but it is not what most of us have been taught to believe – forgiveness simply means to release all negative emotion that has been generated within us as a result of the harmful act of another. When we do this, what most of us now understand to be forgiveness will be a complete and effortless side effect of the real forgiveness process, rather than the troublesome and largely ineffective process most of us currently attempt to engage.

To maximize the potential of this law on our path of healing, and life in general, we have to know *what* we're repenting for or forgiving. We never repent fully for something until we have truly experienced the pain of the suffering we have caused, which is going to be difficult to do if we haven't also gone through the process of forgiveness and felt the often terrifying reality of the suffering that was inflicted upon us by others.

And by the same token, we have to know *what* we are forgiving someone for. One can't fully go through the process of forgiveness until one has felt the suffering that they endured, which is going to be difficult if one hasn't begun to open up to the flow of universal love which itself cannot fully happen whilst one remains in a state of denial (unrepentant) of their own breaches of natural law (harm they have caused to another).

Therefore, forgiveness and repentance are a function of each other and, where we have both participated in and been subject to unresolved transgressions of natural law, we can't do one without the other. You can't forgive what you are in denial even happened, and you can't forgive until you have experienced how much pain was actually caused.

A person with narcissistic traits will, for example, have to forgive the inverted male power expressions that were visited upon him in his earlier co-dependent state, before he will experience the emotional fullness of what he is repenting for.

Generally speaking, the process for transcending one's narcissistic tendencies (inverted male power dynamics) will require engaging the Law of Repentance, whereas transcending one's co-dependencies (which are also driving those inverted male power dynamics) will require engaging the Law of Forgiveness.

One who masters the Law of Forgiveness & Repentance is no longer subject to the Law of Compensation (Karma). Such a state is what Buddhism describes as stepping off the wheel of Karma into the state of Dharma, but natural law is really just g-d's science – we don't need to over-spiritualize it in this way. In fact when we stop doing so, such a state becomes a much more realistic possibility from where we stand.

The Law of Compensation

Also, known as the Law of Karma, the Law of Compensation acts to bring balance to the universe where there has been a transgression of natural law and the Law of Forgiveness & Repentance has not been engaged. It utilizes the Law of Attraction to fulfill its function.

The Law of Compensation is the law which the majority of people experience the effects of the majority of the time – these are those effects/experiences which we generally complain about all the time; the ones we don't like to experience. However, unlike the image often held of Karma, its purpose is not penal, nor does it demand endless reincarnation cycles – there is no vengeful god getting kicks from inflicting suffering, and the law operates on your spirit whether you are physically incarnate or not. The Law of Compensation is an impersonal principle designed to show beings who have free-will what they need to address if they are to cease depleting their condition and begin to improve it. Of all the laws, despite it being responsible for all of our perceived negative experiences, it is actually the one which is the greatest of gifts when we understand how to work with it – it literally exists solely to help us experience more love in our lives.

To maximize the potential of this law on our path of healing, and life in general, we respond to every experience that we would normally not like to experience by first looking at what the experience is trying to show us about our misalignment with natural law, before we take any action in response to the event.

By way of example, say you find yourself getting angry about being repeatedly awoken every day by road-works or a pesky neighbor. The Law of Compensation is trying to alert you to your anger in a safe environment so that you can address the wound which lies behind the anger. The losing your job example earlier in this chapter may also be the Law of Compensation at work – perhaps you are harboring some over-inflated entitlement issues which lead you to cause harm in the world and the Law of Compensation is operating upon you to address them?

If we understood this law, we would know that our attractions will not improve until we engage the process of forgiveness and repentance which is largely what this book is about – creating the conditions in which that can occur.

The Law of Correspondence

Creation is fractal. The microcosm is a reflection of the macrocosm and the macrocosm a reflection of the microcosm. For the purpose of this discussion it offers us both the ability to effect change on a cellular level as part of our own healing processes, and the key to maximizing our capacity as creator-beings once we have stepped into our authentic masculine authority. What we can effect on the micro level we can also effect on the macro level and vice versa.

The Law of Freedom

One's alignment with the other laws, most notably, for the purpose of this discussion, one's capacity to engage the Law of Forgiveness & Repentance, is directly proportionate to one's experience of freedom. For it represents the degree to which one is no longer subject to the Law of Compensation, and is receiving attractions that are in alignment with love and truth.

It is through the Law of Freedom that natural law guarantees that action based on wisdom and taken from a space of love will create sovereignty/freedom (growth), and that action based on ignorance and taken from a space of fear will create slavery/degradation (decline). Everything we do that is driven by ignorance will inevitably create a decline in our present soul condition.

To maximize the potential of this law on our path of healing, and life in general, we ask ourselves, in every situation or relationship where we feel our freedom is limited or being limited, these questions:

1. Who or what do I feel is limiting my experience of freedom?
2. What is it that I am doing in relation to that person or thing that is not granting that person or thing *it's* freedom from me?
3. How are my actions in relation to that person or thing out of alignment with the other laws?

The Law of Contract

Nothing exists in creation that is not operated by a contract.

Whilst there is a core framework of universal natural law that is set in place by the creator of this universe, the vast majority of natural laws (though not those covered in this chapter) have in fact evolved themselves, within creation, based upon that framework. For example there are laws that govern the operation of carbon and there are laws that govern the operation of oxygen. Through the operation of other laws, these substances eventually bonded with each other to create carbon dioxide. A new set of laws was created, within creation, that govern carbon dioxide. The same applies to you – all of the *bona fide* contracts and agreements you create in life are by definition based upon the exercise of your free-will and the free-will of another therefore, unless a party to an agreement has been dishonest, coercive or has withheld important information at the time of their making, all your agreements are themselves natural law. By breaching an agreement that you and another have entered in good faith, you *will* cause harm.

If we are to realign with natural law we must honor the aspects of natural law that we have ourselves created as, albeit unconscious, creator-beings.

Honor your agreements fully. Where you can't honor them fully, renegotiate them before you dishonor them. Do not lie or use mischief in your agreements. Be truthful and transparent when you make agreements. Do not coerce others into agreement with you. Do not continue to honor an agreement where you discover the other has been dishonest, coercive or has withheld important information at the time of its making – this is not an agreement, and you are complicit with the breach of natural law if you continue to honor it with knowledge of the breach.

***

This is the law. The law is love. We stand in violation of it. Love will not return until we realign with the law.

We were never taught what the law is, because no one entrusted with our education knew it either. But once we do know it, what choice will we make? Once we do know it, it is no longer ignorance of the law that creates our personal and worldly circumstances if we act out of alignment with it, it is willful ignorance. And willful ignorance carries a much higher penalty to the soul.

3 MAKING SPACE

You may already be reading this book and saying "I don't have time for all this – I've got bills to pay, mouths to feed… yada, yada." And if you're not already thinking this, you probably will be when something in these pages triggers a subconscious self-preservation mechanism and you want to run for the hills. So I'm going to take a moment to head you off at the pass!

What if you could use natural law to simplify your life tremendously so that you could create for yourself the time and space to both focus on your own evolution, and use your knowledge of the other laws to create the life you have imagined?

It's actually much simpler to do this than you would imagine. Everything we do/create in this world which is out of alignment with natural law creates either a real or a perceived maintenance obligation. If we look at everything in our lives to see where we are expending energy upon creativity and where we are expending energy upon maintenance, we will be able to see just how much of our lives are spent doing things that are not in harmony with natural law. When we can see what that is – and most people currently spend most of their lives on maintenance obligations – we can act to change it.

The goal is to have a life which contains as few maintenance obligations as possible.

As my friend pointed out when first proof-reading this book "doesn't love change the nature of duty while being dutiful?" and "isn't maintenance transcended through love?" And the answer is yes and yes – as we engage the hero's journey to our authentic masculine self-mastery; as we grow in love each day, two things happen, 1. our perception of our maintenance obligations shifts so that we no longer perceive them as the burden they once were (like in the second example below), and 2. We naturally begin to engage only in things that are in alignment with natural law. But until we do embody that degree of love, there are some practical things we can do in our current lives to help make the space for love to emerge.

Examples:
1. If you run a company and find that the vast of majority of your time is spent uncreatively on maintaining the company or engaging tiresome activities, then you can see quite clearly that either what your company does, or how it does it, or both, is out of alignment with natural law.
2. If you see your responsibility as a father or husband (or mother or wife) as a series of maintenance obligations – put a roof over your head, put food on the table, get up in the middle of the night to feed you – then the way you're fulfilling your role is clearly out of alignment with natural law. Whereas if you see your responsibility to your family as an endless opportunity to create more love in everyone's lives then you are most likely fulfilling your role in more alignment with natural law. It's not necessarily one or the other, more a sliding scale.
3. If you see your job as an obligation, i.e. you wouldn't be doing it if it weren't for the pay check, then your participation in that activity is out of alignment with natural law.

We can dissect each of these instances much further by looking at each action we take in life based on whether it is a creative or maintenance-based pursuit and thereby see what of the way I run my business is out of alignment with natural law; what of the way I fulfill my role as father/mother/husband/wife is out of alignment with natural law; what of me and the way I do things, the way I am, the way I perceive the world, is out of alignment with natural law.

Once we have really dissected each area of our life, we need to take some action to change it. If the business is salvageable based on this principle, change the way you do things so that you and everyone who works with you is spending their time creatively. If the business is simply too far out alignment with natural law to do this, sell it or walk away and start doing something creatively entrepreneurial instead. And if we are wise, we will also take this opportunity to engage the relevant natural laws to discover *why* the things in our life have taken the imbalanced form that they have, in order that we can address the cause and prevent them from repeating.

When I first did this in my own life, I did it in emphatic style – I walked away from my business, cancelled every direct debit and standing order, and quit using money altogether. What I didn't do is address my own needs in the process, so it begat a period where, whilst my family and I had everything we absolutely needed, there was a significant lack of resources. It did however give me the instantaneous effect of only having creative pursuits to occupy my time with. With the benefit of hindsight, I would have channeled some of my creative pursuits to providing for my family and I rather than just to serve humanity – I saw these two things as mutually exclusive when in fact they are one and the same. You can apply this principle as gently or vigorously as you feel compelled.

Regardless of how we go about it, if we can make this a new principle for operating in life – to base our future decisions for the choices we make as to where and how to expend our energy on whether our actions will create a maintenance obligation for ourselves or anyone else – we will have a much easier ride. If we create a further maintenance obligation for ourselves we will need to undo it later and we will have made life more difficult for ourselves in the meantime, and if we create one for others we will, under many circumstances, need to later make amends for the further harm we have caused.

A creative life is a low-maintenance life is a simple life – one which gives you all the time you need.

I am reminded of the old adage – "Before enlightenment chop wood, carry water. After enlightenment, chop wood, carry water." Whilst this is true, it is also incomplete. The reality is more like this – "Before enlightenment spend half your time chopping wood and carrying water whilst perceiving it as a maintenance obligation, and the other half trying to chop water and carry wood. After enlightenment spend the same half of your time chopping wood and carrying water without it being a burden, and the other half doing something purely creative!"

The beautiful thing about this is that one man's maintenance obligation is, in the case of purely perceptual maintenance obligations, another's creative passion, so you may just find yourself attracting some new people into your life when you make this your new way of being!

4 WHERE IT ALL WENT WRONG

Picture the scene – it's many tens, possibly hundreds, of millennia hence, and the first human beings are walking the earth. Actually the metaphoric Adam and Eve story is probably not too far from the truth – human beings living in a relatively high state of awareness, knowing who they truly are and having knowledge of the natural loving laws of the universe. Everyone knew that there was always one simple choice in each moment – to honor the law and grow in love, or dishonor the law and decline in love. Some chose wisely, some did not. We are the progeny of those who did not.

As our forebears declined in love, so too did they limit their capacity to perceive truth, because beyond a certain point they even began to act unlovingly toward each other which meant they needed to create false beliefs in order to preserve their sense of self. Emotional wounding ensued and thus began the never-ending cycle described in our introduction – the false self was born en masse.

The false self is everything we incorrectly *think* comprises who and what we are and which, through our identification with it, prevents us from seeing ourselves, the world and others the way they *really* are.

As children we needed the true love of our parents. Which I'm sure would have been lovely but, since by any even partially true definition of love none of us were truly loved by our parents (whether we are ready to accept it yet or not), we had to create some false beliefs to tell ourselves that love was something other than what it really is, so we could pretend that we were loved after all. These beliefs that we created to make ourselves feel we were loved, and which subsequently govern our entire world view and how we relate to others, are false.

So the false self is a psychological construct to mask the emotional pain and terror relating to the unloving experiences we had as a child – a set of inorganic constructs that we developed in the interest of self-preservation from a world which gave us pain and made us terrified of experiencing more pain.

The diagram below describes its structure.

The false-self

The pain sitting behind the false self is actually a series of pain bodies that represent various fractured elements of self, or 'sub-personalities'. At each moment or sequence of events in which great trauma was experienced, we created a separate fracture. It is now our job to collect up and reintegrate each of these fractured aspects of ourselves. There is however one fractured self that is very much in charge of all the others – it is the one which carries our core love wound.

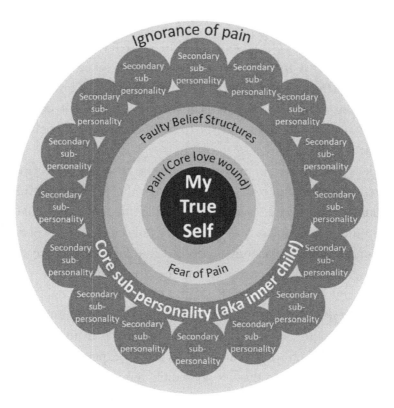

Expanded view of interior behind the false-self

The core love wound is different from every other wound because it is the one we need to be able to heal if we are ever going to fully heal the rest – it is the one that broke our hearts, and which continues to draw the experience of having it broken over and over again as the Law of Compensation draws endless experiences to us in an attempt to show us that it is there so we can heal it and return to love… if only we knew and applied this law. It is also the one which can't easily be healed because we don't possess the capacity for the degree of self-love it requires. This is because the trauma that it is holding has robbed us of that capacity – it is *its own* worst enemy, and so far in your life it has been *your* worst enemy too. This entire process of true personal healing is based on you changing that – the negative influences of the archetypes, collective masculine/feminine and inter-dimensional interference that we will discuss shortly, will all fall away when you do.

Each secondary sub-personality is its own fractal of the whole, carrying in a sense its own piece of your soul essence (true self), its own pain (from some specific life trauma), its own fear of experiencing that pain, and its own belief structures it created in order to cope. Collectively this dirty soup creates a serious wall of ignorance!

So let's look at how, in practical terms, the false-self was formed.

Firstly, you came into this world through the veil of forgetfulness and, unless your mother only experienced loving emotions while you were in utero, and unless you had a very conscious birth experience with her, and unless she truly embodied the divine love from which you came, you received a seriously big shock to your system.

Then, unless this love was present and unfailing throughout your early years, your early childhood experiences were extremely painful. You are wired for love, it is what you are made from, and if you didn't receive it fully, or you also had to endure experiences that were explicitly unloving, then this was incredibly traumatic. So traumatic in fact that you have denied that any of it really happened – this is the real core stuff.

Usually before the age of two, but sometimes a little later if we did not experience much aggression in the home, this pain has become so great that we became terrified of life; so great that we became terrified of a future in which we were certain to experience more of it, that we engaged our primal survival drive to preserve ourselves against that pain.

It began with the creation of stories which would explain away the injustices of life in a way that wouldn't require us to feel the pain they wrought – these stories took the form of false beliefs and more specifically false notions of what love really is, so that we could tell ourselves that our parents loved us, when really they never had the capacity to do so.

With a false belief structure now in place, we were protected from the pain, but in doing so we made ourselves ignorant to the truth of ourselves and of life for the first time. This ignore-ance of truth was the foundation for our growth into a being that was variously broken and without the capacity to perceive how to fix him/herself. We chose survival over the truth. Our core wounded self had now been formed.

Our childhood experiences now begin to really shape our behavior. Every area where one or both of our parents were not in complete balance with themselves created a corresponding co-dependency in us (lots of them usually), for example, an over-giving mother that creates co-dependency and nurtures false expectations and entitlement, or a controlling father who stunts the development of the use of our will or capacity for creativity.

Being long since cut off from our source of divine energy, we adopt coping mechanisms in the form of physical addictions (to numb the pain), emotional addictions (victimhood, anger, judgments, accusations, control dramas, etc. – to subconsciously acquire that energy from other people), and spiritual addictions (religion and other non-temporal beliefs) as a means of justifying our false-light actions.

This is inverted male power – we apply those coping mechanisms in alignment with the co-dependencies that were created in us. For example, the child with the entitlement issue will use his emotional addictions to get what he feels entitled to from others. The broken child who now lacks the will for original creativity will use her emotional addictions to balance the scales of unfairness she feels exists. None of this seems wrong to us because our imbalances are telling us that what is right and just is something other than what is really right and just – we are out of alignment with natural law so our perception of the truth is dirty.

Through both continuing childhood trauma arising from circumstances beyond our control, and further childhood and adult trauma arising as a result of our having expressed our emotional coping mechanisms in the world, further sub-personalities are created every time we experience a traumatic event and do not process that trauma there and then – which we don't because we have been taught not to. This is not a literal picture, but essentially a piece of our soul is fractured from itself and boxed away inside its own layers of pain, fear of pain, set of beliefs to translate the trauma, and a whole new layer of ignorance. Some people have many fractured aspects of themselves to reintegrate, and some will have fewer but perhaps more significant ones.

As the years go by without processing or addressing any of this, the false self solidifies itself.

We have been in denial of it since its creation (it is our self-created self-preservation tool so denial of it is fundamental to the continuity of its existence), but having now lived each day as a false self, creating a lot of harm to both ourselves and others in the process, as each day passes it becomes harder and harder to accept the truth of our distorted creation. Over time a very thick wall of denial forms around everything (that's the big black line around the outer edge of the diagram earlier in this chapter).

Inter-dimensional interference

What makes it infinitely more challenging to see and overcome the strong-hold of the false self, is the fact that there are endless beings, in other planes of existence, who are also reliant upon incarnate human beings as their energetic food source. They outnumber us humans significantly, and their very survival is incumbent on our remaining wounded, because one who is in balance within themselves – carrying no emotional trauma and being aligned with the truth – is impervious to such interference, and if we all healed ourselves, that food source would dry up. Unfortunately however, very few people are balanced, aligned with truth, and without trauma, so for almost all of us, inter-dimensional interference *is* informing great chunks of our experience. For many, almost all of their experience is governed this way, whether they care to accept it or not. In fact the more resistance one has to this statement, the more interference they are likely experiencing.

These beings fall into two broad categories – spirits (former physical human beings loitering in the astral plane), and other entities (non-human forms that have no connection to source and require to be fed by those who do), and they influence or control our thoughts, words or actions in order to obtain their meal.

Have you ever had nasty thoughts that you feel aren't normal? Have you ever found yourself more emotionally triggered by something than usual? Do you often find yourself physically tired, weak or lethargic? Do you have a physical addiction that you want to shake but can't? These are almost always all examples of inter-dimensional interference, and there are many more.

Challenges with overcoming physical addictions, from smoking cigarettes to alcohol, drugs, sex or porn, are almost always the result of one or more spirits attaching themselves to the addict to feed their own physical addictions after passing. Other more sinister influences, like implanting certain thoughts or even taking over large chunks of cognitive capacities, are usually the reserve of entities. *All* mental illness is supercharged by such interference.

Whilst I never had any doubt that such things existed and had some influence over my life, it was not until I learnt how to scan my field to observe and remove for myself what was actually interfering with me that I became aware of just how significant this influence really is. I discovered everything from portals to other galaxies that presumably entities were using to travel through and interfere with me when I was not aware, to serpent-like creatures attached to major energy centers, to billions of artificial nano-bot spiders... and much more besides.

Other types of entities operate through, or use the force of, the archetypes. One such entity that has birthed through the Magician archetype, for example, has become the most powerful and diabolical living entity anywhere in the sphere of human influence. It is he who drives, and whose inverted male power is utilized for, amongst other things, the brutalization of innocence via pedophilic practices and the satanic ritualistic blood sacrifice of children and babies. The same power which has been used to invert kundalini energy as the basis for the planet-wide control grid which currently imprisons the minds, bodies and spirits of the vast majority of the human species. The inverted kundalini energy that results from such practices becomes his direct food source, which he in turn feeds to all the emotionally wounded people who will take it, perpetuating the story and his grip on power over endless generations on the physical plane. There are literally billions of such entities endlessly vying for human life force energy.

In a very real sense it is the existence of our false selves that invites the dark-side in – the dark-side can only manipulate that which is out of alignment with love, and only your false self is out of alignment with love. Your false self may have originally been a self-defense mechanism, but it has become quite the opposite – it is permissioning the draining of your life force via inter-dimensional interference; it is enabling you to serve the dark-side without you knowing it; and it is driving your expressions of inverted male power. It is not our human energy which is 'inverted' – our own energy is hijacked for food and another put in its place. In a very real sense, where we are expressing inverted male power, the dark-side is truly living in us as us. This is the eternal battle between good and evil and your body is the battlefield because you have unknowingly vacated it.

None of this is something that anyone ever ought to take as gospel. Witness this for yourself and take steps to address what you witness – there are plenty of people who teach people how to perceive and remove spirits and entities from their field. Anyone who has even the slightest sensitivity will easily perceive it for themselves when shown how.

Nor is any of this something that anyone should be afraid of – it's not going to kill us, and we are each *far* more powerful than every entity in existence combined, but we have to face the reality before we can, very easily, free ourselves of such interference. And our experience of inter-dimensional interference is, in reality, a result of the Law of Compensation at work again, so you could even say that such interference is yet another beautiful gift which we can use to show us what remains to be healed within us.

We can never allay blame for our circumstances on spirits or entities that are trying to control us. A spirit or entity can only control someone through their emotions, and specifically only those that they are avoiding feeling. Any extra-terrestrial/inter-dimensional interference you may experience is a direct result of your own refusal to feel an emotion that you have been hiding from – this is your choice and you can end it any time, by making the choice to feel *everything*... no matter what.

5 HOW THIS WAS CREATED IN US

The masculine influence

So let's get straight down to the crux of the matter shall we, which is also both the inspiration for the name of this book, and the reason why I call it inverted male power.

Any expression of inverted male power is a direct reflection of our own innate powerlessness, which we perpetuate subconsciously to hide *from* that powerlessness. The more we express inverted male power, the more powerless we really are.

For pretty much any boy who was born into a household where another man was present, unless that man really was himself the balanced representation of divine masculine embodied (a rarity to say the least), he came face to face with some level of inverted male power. Often he will avoid being on the receiving end of it until he begins to show signs of becoming a threat, at perhaps around 18-24 months old. At that point he made the safest and simplest choice he could – to energetically neuter himself of his own natural, and as yet undeveloped, divine masculine power capabilities in order to cease being a threat to the male figure and align more deeply with the nurturing mother. I did this, you did this, we all did this – yes, in every way that it actually mattered, we effectively chopped our dicks off.

Some young boys didn't of course have a nurturing mother, but they still neutered themselves in order to cease being a threat to the male figure. And some young boys didn't have any male influence in the home at all, but they still came face to face with it at some point, and they never anyway developed their own divine masculine power because there was no role model upon which to base that development, and/or because the mother figure they did have was, as a single mother, less than perfect herself, and fundamentally incapable of nurturing that aspect in him.

From here on in, that little boy, whatever his story, needed to find some other way to develop some kind of power that would allow him to survive the circumstances of his childhood and of life in general.

For my part, I had an unconditionally loving mother and a police officer father who was moral, just and kind-hearted – sounds like a pretty good deal, right? And, despite a few obvious chinks, this is how I saw them both for the majority of my life – holding them in extremely high regard (in fact I still do, just in a more truthful way)... but this was not the whole story, and if you have similarly positive views on your own parents, I guarantee this wasn't your whole story either.

My father, righteous and kind hearted as he was, carried so much trauma from his own childhood that he had developed a significant amount of inverted male power of his own in order to cope, and then joined the police force which is itself *the* societal metaphor of narcissistic inverted male power gone mad.

So, just as in the general dynamic I describe above, I neutered myself of my masculine power at a very early age so as not to be a threat to my father, and to align more deeply with my mother.

I was, like most of us men at such an age, afraid of power – because I was given a false reflection of what power actually is.

My father certainly wasn't as bad as many in terms of actually attacking or harming me directly – this was definitely the least of my problems, but he would criticize and interrogate – usually in the form of humor, which we were all encouraged to see as an admirable quality, so as to mask the despotic nature of the real energy behind the expressions, and it certainly did serve to make me feel small – ashamed. He also instilled a fear of making noise; making mess – there was no real capacity for self-expression in the home. I, like every other small child who had their divinity snatched from them (in whatever small or large way and by whatever means was unique to their circumstance), had only two choices, having no natural basis remaining from which to develop authentic masculine power following their self-inflicted castration – either to remain as pure food for their father (and in the case of many, also their mother) and potentially every other human being they would meet in life, or to adopt similar tactics to those which the father himself used to steal power from them and the rest of the world around him. I have not met a single man, and far too few women, who chose to do the former.

The tactics I chose to adopt were 1. The very same critical, interrogatory tactics he used, and 2. The energetic opposite of this particular tactic – aloofness – the act of stealing energy from others by subconsciously manufacturing a state of unhappiness and remaining silent when others inquired as to the reason, or by simply not sharing information about the things one is doing that people are interested in; drawing them into giving their attention and energy for more extended periods of time. I used the latter to slow the energetic feeding tide and balance the vampirical scales with my father (and anyone else who would use the same tactic on me), and would later use the former to vampirize from the rest of humanity – both men and women, including my own mother – in search of reclaiming the energy that my own innate powerlessness was unable to acquire any other way. This is just one face of what I call observable inverted male power.

You may have developed and expressed your observable inverted male power traits in different ways…

Perhaps your father's most dominant inverted male power game was aloofness? Then you will likely have become interrogatory to balance the scales with him, and aloof yourself as a means of vampirizing the rest of the world?

Perhaps your father's most dominant inverted male power game was aggression/intimidation? Then you will likely have played the victim to balance the scales with him, and become aggressive/intimidating yourself (or continued to play the victim) as a means of vampirizing the rest of the world?

Perhaps your father's most dominant inverted male power game was victimhood? Then you will likely have become aggressive/intimidating to balance the scales with him, and played the victim yourself (or continued to be aggressive/intimidating) as a means of vampirizing the rest of the world?

Perhaps you actually learnt your own tactics from your mother rather than your father? Or perhaps you took on a mix of several or all of these? Regardless how it played out for you, you were doing so in response to the underlying dynamic of powerlessness initiated by your subconscious choice to neuter yourself. These dynamics have many more intricate faces of course which we'll look at in more detail in Chapter 7.

As alluded to earlier, most women also develop one or more of these tactics to defend against a world gone mad, but they do so in response to this core energetic masculine debasement of natural divine power.

And so the abused becomes the abuser – expressing inverted male power, not only in defense of that expression from others, but aggressively toward others too. Yes – victimhood and aloofness are also acts of aggression when they are done with the subconscious intent to steal, which is always.

But this is the easy part of the inverted male power game to see – it is visible; it can be observed with the five senses by anyone of good will; and it can be deconstructed and overcome with relative ease as soon as we are willing to be truthful with ourselves. Later in this book we will look at exactly how to do that. The more challenging aspects to see however are the covert expressions of inverted male power. These require a more skilled eye to observe, and a much greater degree still of truthfulness with ourselves if we are to address them in any meaningful way. How these aspects play out we will also cover shortly, along with how to deconstruct those aspects of ourselves too.

A mother's touch

It is taboo to speak ill of mothers in this world, but unfortunately that taboo is suppressing more honest emotional expression and therefore contributing more to the dysfunction of society than any other. The truth is that the majority of mothers are responsible for far more emotional wounding to their children than fathers and the rest of society put together. This is not about turning people against their mothers, it is quite the opposite in fact – it is about acknowledging that there will never be any change in the ways of the world, nor any clearing of any emotional dysfunction of people and society generally, until we begin to do three things. 1. To be honest and truthful… about everything, especially those things we don't want to be honest and truthful about, 2. To repent for the harm we have caused (*as* mothers, fathers and in general), and 3. To forgive the harm caused to us by others (*by* our mothers, fathers and in general).

The greatest harm anyone has ever caused us is almost certainly our own mothers, and we need to move beyond denying that harm, to seeing what it really is, to feeling deeply what that has done to us and grieving, before we can even begin to forgive – we can't forgive what we deny even took place, and we can't accept what actually took place until we suspend all our ideas of who we think our mother to be. Only after engaging such a process will we actually be able to love our mothers in a clean and true way for the very first time. This really is the only truly loving action we could display toward our mothers.

We all carry a core love wound which is central to our relationship with the feminine. The core love wound is largely based around the hidden grief of how we were abandoned by our mothers; and thus by the feminine. This core abandonment wound exists in almost everyone to varying degrees. It begins at our conception, where for nine months we are a sponge for the emotional state of our mother – what she feels, we feel. If she is stressed, so are we. If she is sorrowful, angry, afraid or anxious, so are we. So by the time we are born we have already developed a certain expectation of what the world will be like. This is probably a god-send, for if we were to transition directly from the field of expansive pure divine love to 'the world' without any 'warming up', it would surely be even more traumatic. Nonetheless, when we are born, we are at best met with an emotionally available unconditionally loving (natural, not divine, love) mother, in which case the damage is very small, and if it stopped here, easily reversed, or at worst we are met with an emotionally unavailable aggressor, in which case the damage can be huge. But this abandonment wound *will* grow significantly, and our mothers *will* be responsible for creating other wounds throughout our childhood to accompany it wherever she, no matter how apparently loving, has never faced her own emotional pain of abandonment. Whilst we may often develop our inverted male power tactics elsewhere, the vast majority if not all of our expressions of it are driven at their heart by these core mother wounds.

If a woman does not face her own pain caused by her own parents and thereby overcome the emotional trauma that she herself carries, then when she chooses to have a child it is inevitable that she will train the child to meet for her the unhealthy emotional needs that result from her own trauma – in fact it is also inevitable that on some level this was a substantial yet unconscious part of her true motivation for actually having a child in the first place. That is of course very dirty, but almost every parent does it.

The ways in which mothers unfold trauma within us are literally infinite, thus it is impossible to cover every eventuality here. Nor is it necessary – this book is about showing you how to map and thereby transcend your own imbalances, so you can figure it all out for yourself. Nonetheless, to highlight just how substantially even seemingly wonderful mothers can cause more trauma in us than anyone else, my own experience serves as a perfect example – my mother was unconditionally loving, fulfilled all my physical needs with grace, and was one of those few very special people who never adopted any passive or aggressive strategies for stealing energy from others – she was, by society's definition, pretty close to the perfect mother. And yet the majority of my trauma came from her, in fact I would never have developed the wounds that caused me to express the inverted male power I picked up from my father at all were it not for her.

Unconditionally loving and present as she was, she was physically over-giving (a trait which she, and the rest of the world, was raised to view as an admirable quality), but more significantly, her own childhood traumas made her co-dependent, so she needed from another a sense of worth and identity. Since, because of her own imbalances and her unwillingness to address them, a woman is only able to attract as a partner someone who would consolidate her current state, my father only served to engender the opposite of self-worth and a healthy sense of identity (i.e. by requiring her to validate, and subject herself to, a great amount unloving behavior). For such a woman, a child offers the only opportunity they will ever get for a blank canvas from which to mold a human being to meet their subconscious, unmet & unhealthy needs that they were unable to get from their partners or anyone else. Such a mother will invariably, on the one hand, train their child to meet their unhealthy emotional needs, and on the other, generate an overinflated sense of entitlement in the child by being over-giving toward them (usually making the child a vampirical twat when they come to engaging relationship with others when they find that other people don't do the same thing). But here's where it gets really nasty – because such children have become the basis of the mothers identity, the mother never allows the child their own energetic independence when they would naturally start to choose it for themselves (at around two years old).

So the core abandonment wound suffered by most every human

being from their mother is supercharged in such an instance by 1. Making the child unhealthily dependent upon the mother, then 2. Essentially ripping away the rug by sending the child to nursery or school where none of the dependencies the mother created in the child would be fulfilled, and 3. Doing the above whilst holding on for dear life, out of their own neediness, to the unhealthy energetic cord that makes the child subconsciously need the mother all the time whilst she is not there. For me, this had tremendous repercussions, which lasted well over 30 years, on the lives of many people. Some variation of this dynamic exists within probably one third to one half of the male population.

Boys who receive this kind of motherly love go out into the world with two main subconscious false beliefs about women, 1. That they will abandon you in the end (and not just abandon you but love you completely and then rip it all away, and probably not let you go gracefully when they do), and 2. That they are responsible for fulfilling your needs. Why? Because the mother has been over-giving, so as a result the child develops a false sense of entitlement of women – if the mother would fulfill all their physical and emotional needs, to an unhealthy degree, then the expectation will be that all women should do the same.

So what about the other end of the spectrum?

Perhaps your mother was more narcissistic, or at least expressed more narcissistic traits, than co-dependent ones?

Perhaps she was very controlling and demanding of your attention?

Perhaps she didn't display much patience or empathy?

Perhaps your endless efforts to please her never yielded the praise or validation you so desperately sought?

Perhaps you were nervous or anxious in her presence – afraid to take her on for fear that she would get mad at you?

Perhaps she would never back down from a fight – you would always lose, so you gave up trying and stuck with trying to please her… which you never could?

Perhaps she was easily offended and regularly pulled the "you don't appreciate me as a mother" or "you don't love me because if you did you would do what I wanted" card?

Perhaps you developed a great sense of inadequacy and became very self-doubting when nothing you did yielded the praise you knew you deserved?

Perhaps she was charismatic, kind, forgiving, graceful and happy in public, but as soon as you were behind closed doors broke out the critical and diminishing behavior?

Perhaps she was a master at manipulating your emotions to make you feel like her needs took priority and that you were responsible for meeting them?

Perhaps you felt the overwhelming sense that you were a failure when you didn't meet those needs adequately, which was always an impossibility, and for which "sorry" would never compensate?

And perhaps you were made to feel ungrateful for not being ok with all this?

And perhaps your experience of any or all of these narcissistic traits made you into a co-dependent man with low self-esteem, self-worth and little capacity for real self-love, who still aims to please everyone with little awareness of, or respect for, your own real needs?

Or perhaps you took the 'if you can't beat 'em, join 'em' path, taking on some or all of those traits for yourself in order to traverse a seemingly unfair world – maybe she is proud that you now reflect well on her as the worldly successful energetic rapist you have become, and so you now demand that adoration from other women too, or maybe you just demand that regardless?

Irrespective of how the dynamic with your mother looked for you, one thing is constant – you were royally fubar., and inevitably developed a healthy dose of inverted male power as a result, having therefore equally solid foundations for perpetrating the same or similar abuses on the rest of the women you meet in your life.

But whilst it is true that mothers (and women in general) perpetrate the vast majority of the harm toward men that causes those same men to later act in the same way that the collective feminine is already wired to hate men for, it is also true that mothers only do this because they were themselves distorted by inverted male power. It is a vicious circle and the truth is that both men and women are now all just living this dynamic as cyclical 'victims' of it, with all the original perpetrators having long left the scene.

So who is going to do something about it? Well many of the women of our generation are already stepping up to do something about it, but they can only go so far without a man by their side willing to do it with them. Hence this book.

It is nothing more or less than *our* denial of the pain *we* have endured that now causes us to subconsciously perpetuate the male dominance paradigm – *our* denial. The only question is, are we going to accept ourselves fully to end it once and for all?

As we continue, you should begin to be able to understand the nature of your own familial dynamics and how you can begin to accept them, feel the real damage they caused, and forgive them for yourself. When you do, you will actually love your mother cleanly for the very first time!

School and the formative years

In addition to our parents, school is also where we learn what is acceptable by society. And we get taught that there is an acceptable range of emotional expression. You're allowed to be happy, and you're allowed to be sad, but if you go past a certain threshold in either direction, it's time for the medication... there's something wrong with you. This is probably the most significant and damaging societal meme that is impressed upon us during school, as it solidifies and legitimizes the tendency toward emotional suppression that we've already picked up in the home.

The manner in which school affects our development of inverted male power is very much dependent upon the types of trauma, or lack thereof, we have already developed to date. Where we have experienced quite a lot of, particularly mother-induced, trauma to that point, the transition to school may not feel so bad – if you weren't so sensitive and empathic at the time you began school to experience it as the warzone many do, it's likely that your innocence had already been raped out of you by that time.

If you were sensitive as a boy, school was brutal – it was when you got to 'catch up' in one shocking hit with everyone who had already had their innocence raped out of them. And by the time we get to high school, gone is any remaining innocence – this is the military, pure and simple… whoever you are. My high school experience probably looked pretty awesome to anyone looking in – I had a lot of very cool friends, I was in the top percentiles in both academic and popularity stakes – it was as good as it could have been, but energetically it was still brutal.

I was the school drug dealer – or one of them. All the free weed you can imagine at 14 years old hardly helped my brain development! I was high for most of my end of school exams. But even with this and all that it entailed, I was still a pussy inside.

Were you bullied or the bully?

If you were the bully, you had likely already developed a great amount of your inverted male power. If you were bullied, probably you were either slower to develop it, or you developed the more passive expressions of it – victimhood and/or aloofness.

It was actually the shock of being sent to school in the manner I was that was the principal nexus point for my development of inverted male power. The reason why this was the critical point in my own development was because of the state of abject shock that it instilled as a result of an unhealthy degree of motherly love which was physically ripped away, with unhealthy attachments left in place, upon being sent to school.

By the time I reached high school (at 12 years old) I was already in the groove of both ends of the inverted male power game – in my first year I once agreed to go out with five girls at the same time, without telling any of them about each other, essentially just to be cruel and get a laugh out of it – I thought it would be funny to watch them have their hearts broken.

And I once bullied a boy terribly, who was also my after-school friend whose house I would play at most days, just because others were doing it and it was an easy way to generate some sense of self-power – I felt no remorse in this at the time.

And I bore the brunt of equally brutal happenings myself.

And I once perpetrated a great many other things besides…

But we simply cannot deflect responsibility for the harm we have caused by blaming it on our parents. As unfair as it may sometimes feel, natural law holds us accountable for *all* expressions of our free will at whatever age and regardless of what we have experienced as children – it is necessary in order to maintain balance in the universe. Recognizing this, accepting the as yet inconceivable extent of its bearing over our lives, repenting for what we need to, forgiving others for what we have had the courage to face, and choosing to be the fully-expansive emotional beings that we are so that our natural law compass starts pointing north again, is the task in hand. The Natural Law of Compensation is the 'in yer face' gift we have never noticed which is designed for us to use to help guide us through the process – when we understand it, we can use it to chart our course out of the woods.

***

We really need to take a good hard look at what we call education – the current model that most of us experienced taught us nothing except militarization – it taught the art of rape, and it taught us how to be raped as gracefully as possible. But more important than this, as it relates to the topic of this book, is that we need to not only look at the types of environment we send our children to, but also develop the awareness that no child should ever be forced to go somewhere s/he is not ready to go to, be it daycare, nursery, school or otherwise… ever. As parents *we*, not the state, have the responsibility to nurture our children, and nurturing involves fulfilling our children's physical, emotional and spiritual needs in a healthy and balanced way. Whilst it is not unreasonable for a child to go to school, if the child is ready to do so, it is not only unreasonable but morally reprehensible and unimaginably harmful for a child to be forced to do so when s/he is not ready. Nor is there a one-size-fits-all environment that suits all children. A child should go to the school that suits him/her, if/when s/he decides s/he is ready and chooses that for him/herself. If we can be mindful that this will always happen at different ages for different children, and that it will happen a lot later, or never at all, if a child's has unhealthy co-dependencies with its parents, then we might just start to shift this brutal dystopian meme toward more nurturing societal values.

What did you experience at school that developed or cemented your inverted male power dynamics? What did you perpetrate on others that created a significant karmic debt for yourself? What have you done since that time to add to that debt? Remember, our karmic debt increases with every unloving thought, word or deed we have ever thought, spoken or enacted, and it doesn't decrease by paying it back with random acts of kindness, it remains steadfast until you wipe it clean by facing the fear of feeling, and then feeling, the horrific extent of what you have done.

Puberty

This is where two things happen related to trauma:

Firstly, you get to find out just how sexually fucked up you had already been by observing the degree to which sexual imbalances expressed themselves as they came online – how much sexual depravity did your mind then (and later) express? How much were you denied genuine touch and affection as a baby and child? How much were your parents own sexual insecurities thrust upon you as a baby/child? And if you happen to have been sexually abused to boot... well, this must have been a real bitch of a time for you – it was for the rest of us already!

Secondly, in the cauldron which is high school, you get to develop a whole new set of sexual wounds which you will carry through life –

usually building upon the sexual distortions you already carried from your parents as above.

During puberty, whatever your core mother wound is gets supercharged by misunderstood sexual energy. It is misunderstood principally because the natural attachment of a mother to a child after birth takes place principally through the sacral chakra, which is also one of the two main energy centers responsible for our sense of sexuality. Whether our mothers held on to that attachment in an unhealthy way, or whether they never really nurtured it sufficiently in the first place, and almost always one of these is the case, they created an imbalance in a major sexual center. So this is the time when you begin to really anchor the same relationship template you have with your mother as a significant part of your own modus operandi for your relationship with women. This relationship template is influenced by other things as well of course – what you have witnessed in terms of how your father (or male figure) relates to the feminine, the collective masculine field and the pain bodies of the archetypes to name but a few, but the key influential factor is the relationship with your mother.

Additionally, if an unhealthy attachment does exist between parent and child – be it mother and son or father and daughter – at the time puberty arrives, then there is also most likely an incestual component to the relationship. A covert exchange of sexual energy is taking place which the parties are usually oblivious to. This dynamic quite scarily accounts, in some way, for somewhere approaching half of all child/parent relationships.

The collective masculine and the collective feminine

We men carry this very deep rooted wound that the masculine is bad – from inverted male power-based fathers, to general societal reflections, to the whole masculine morphogenetic field being spread thick with shame, everything in life has reflected and strengthened this. The masculine collective really does, mostly subconsciously but nonetheless significantly, feel the hatred of the feminine collective.

New agey circles paint the masculine as lesser; that intelligence is wrong or dirty (not the sacred masculine creation principle it is) because it is somehow not heartful enough; and that the 'goddess rising' is the name of the game when it is mostly just feminism rebooted. It's hardly surprising that the sexes are in lockdown from each other.

The influence of the collective masculine and feminine over our lives is much bigger than we might expect. In fact in hindsight I would even go as far as to say that a major aspect of *why* I always settled for women that I felt were either not right for me or clearly unable to meet my natural needs, was significantly influenced by the collective male shame I felt as part of the male collective and lack of worth/value I felt toward men from the female collective – it was an irrational lack of self-worth not seemingly driven by my own wounding.

This only changed for me when, by some act of grace for which I will remain eternally grateful every moment of my existence, a woman walked into my life one day that was so right, so perfect, so worthy of me that she soon drew out all of this shit from me like poison from a wound. She is the most important woman I will ever meet; she gave me experiences that were both more beautiful than anything I had ever even imagined and more painful than words exist to describe – together we face it all. Our mothers may be the principle cause of our inverted male power, but if we truly desire it, we will attract a goddess who can truly help us heal it… together.

It's an archetype thing

The definition of an archetype, as evolved from Jungian psychology, is a collectively inherited unconscious idea, pattern of thought, image, etc., that creates repeating behavioral patterns. But really we can expand on this. What is not often discussed in the conversation around archetypes, is that the archetypal forms are not in fact purely mental constructs, but emotional ones in that they also appear to gather and hold the sum total of the emotional output of all human experience here on earth. Humanity's collective emotional body (which at present is essentially the same thing as calling it its pain body) is therefore held by, or at the very least attached to, the archetypal forms. This includes all those memes, stories and the related emotional pain and trauma described above that exists between the masculine and feminine – their influence is what perpetuates/fuels the abject shame and other emotional injuries that exist between the masculine and feminine collectives.

Having drawn in all that emotional experience down through the ages, the archetypal forms carry an inordinate amount of power, strengthening the repetitive behavioral patterns here on the physical plane. Every one of us is influenced by these collective pain bodies in our daily experience of life until such time as we are able to fully integrate and release that pain.

The process of healing and becoming whole again, it seems, is ultimately one of connecting to and integrating the pain bodies of the archetypes. And, given that our relationship with the archetypes is a circular feedback loop, as we heal ourselves, we heal the archetypal pain bodies themselves and thus relieve the burden on the collective at the same time. But this is something that happens naturally on its own when we have developed beyond a given point. This chapter is provided for understanding only, not to be another thing you have to do.

The Warrior

For the men reading this – what follows is one of the most important insights in this book. For the women reading this – what follows is the real original story of why we men have brutalized you down through the ages, and thus what continues to fuel the feminine's own brutal behavior toward the masculine. Please try to understand it, for your understanding will help the men around you to soften and transform through this work... which is truly to your greatest benefit. It will also show you how you too have been empowering the abuse against you down through the ages so that you have the knowledge to cease empowering it.

One of the principal archetypes which has been responsible for the male domination paradigm is the Warrior. But here's the thing...

Like every archetype, the qualities of the Warrior are indifferent – they simply evolve based on the emotional expression of we humans. Since our natural state is one of love, it is the Warriors natural state too – to protect the feminine; to love her, not fight her. The problem arose at the time of our collective fall from grace, at which point we men, emotionally insecure creatures that we subsequently became, always required thereafter a love that was certain. At a given point in time, as the collective body of human emotional experience repeatedly reflected to the male collective the experience of *not* having received the everlasting love from the feminine, a sense of global abandonment by the feminine grew. The Warrior has, ever since then, been effectively controlling men to fight *with* the feminine to win that love back.

If we as men are ever going to become whole again and end this mutant story, we must connect with the Warrior within, integrate its entirely indifferent archetypal qualities fully, and channel its energy to have its immense power fight for us (for love) in return for our love, *not* the love of another. The Warrior desires, because of the reflection of the male collective, a love that is certain – and we ourselves are the only place it can get that kind of love. The only reason this all went wrong in the first place is because it never experienced in another a love that was certain and the male collective at the time did not know how to provide it for themselves. Such an integration is a naturally occurring process once we step into our authentic masculine power, which is itself a natural outcome of the process described in Chapter 9.

When enough of us, both men and women, have integrated the pain bodies held by the archetypes they will be released – they will literally cease to exist, and thereby cease to feed the on-going paradigm in the rest of our species. And it will get exponentially easier for those that follow as those who blaze the trail lessen the collective pain that stands in the way. So you goddesses can actively participate in ending the male domination paradigm as well, but then you already are… in far greater numbers than us men, hence the reason for this book!

There are many men who have come face to face with their inverted male power and ceased to express it (many never learnt how to express it very well so it was easier for them), but to not then step into one's true divine masculine authority is an act, or non-act, of fear. The Warrior needs to learn how to love for love instead of fight for love. Most men have not integrated the true nature of their Warrior spirit which is why they cannot do this.

The Warrior is not the only archetype, but he is the one principally responsible for the state of affairs which this book addresses, hence why a far greater focus is placed here. If you are interested, or you find yourself encountering other major archetypal memes on your own journey, there is much information available on this subject to make sense of your experiences.

The Alchemist

Beyond the historic archetypes that have long existed, there are several 'new' archetypes that have birthed in the collective field over recent decades precisely to aid our progress of collective healing and transcendence… but we are interested in one of these for now – the Alchemist. Unlike the other archetypes, the Alchemist is *not* a driving force behind the inverted male power game, rather it represents a typically unembodied aspect of ourselves that will aid in its undoing.

The Alchemist essentially offers us the tools and skill set to 'alchemize' all of the other archetypes within us in order that we may transcend their grip over us, birth ourselves in a new earth, and clean the collective field of their respective pain bodies for others to follow. In this context alchemizing means to balance the positive and negative polarities of each archetype that you embody.

None of this chapter is something you need to engage consciously if it feels too much – we are simply describing here what is actually happening on a macro scale so that you understand the effect of the personal work you do on the collective level. It is not necessary to contextualize it in this fashion if it doesn't work for you. Alchemizing the archetypes within you is something that happens entirely on its own once you have activated your own inner alchemist, but an understanding of the process will probably help you translate your experiences, hence its inclusion in this book. It did for me anyway... once I experienced it all for myself! We do however look at how to use internal alchemy for personal healing in Chapter 9.

Soul Individuation

As controversial as this may sound, your soul is not your soul... not only yours anyway. This particular topic is one that many have an opinion on, but it doesn't require an opinion – it is something that can be known via one's direct experience when one's awareness has expanded their capacity to feel deeper realities to a great enough degree.

Prior to first incarnation, our soul existed in a perfect union state. It had no self-awareness. It's masculine and feminine aspects were in complete balance but, just as we describe in Chapter 2, everything in the universe is dualistic and everything in the universe has polarity. The soul is no exception. Self-awareness arose when it first incarnated as two halves – one usually masculine and the other usually feminine. From this point on, it could know itself.

Of course, both the masculine and feminine aspects of the soul (of which you are one) possess the capacity for balance within themselves, but neither of those halves will ever attain a complete union state until they are reunited. That does not have to happen during a physical incarnation, but it can.

So with all this in mind, it should be easy to imagine that there must have been a great sense of loss from the very first moment that the soul became self-aware – the very first self-aware experience it ever had was the experience of separation from its feminine/masculine counterpart. Though this was not a trauma event insofar as it didn't cause the individuated you to fracture off any piece of yourself, like with other trauma events, it *is* a core emotional driving force insofar as the sense of original loss that occurred will supercharge any related trauma we do experience in life. A related trauma being anything that relates to loss, abandonment or rejection by a member or members of the opposite sex.

It should also be easy to see now *why* the proverbial fall from grace, which caused the Warrior to take the nose dive he did, occurred to our species – the scales of inter-sex harmony were already imbalanced by the sense of original loss, which was fine when we were evolved enough to recognize ourselves and live in harmony with the other, but when the veil of forgetfulness descended following our self-imposed fall from grace, things changed significantly.

We will each only know this to be true for ourselves when we have felt it for ourselves and moved through enough of our fear of the feminine (or masculine if you're a woman) that this just becomes a known experiential aspect of who we are, which will absolutely happen when we do go through the process this book calls us toward… until then, you'll just have to take my word for it!

This section may seem to take the view that homosexuality is not in alignment with natural law. This is not the case. Whilst every soul does indeed carry masculine and feminine qualities, some souls are more masculine and some more feminine. Where the tendency away from equal balance, in either direction, is sufficient in size, it may indeed incarnate as two male, or two female, forms. That is not to say that everyone who believes they are homosexual is actually homosexual at the soul level, just as those who believe they are heterosexual may not necessarily be heterosexual at the soul level. You won't actually know this for sure until all your emotional wounding respecting the opposite sex has been resolved.

6 HOW I MADE IT WORSE, AND HOW YOU MAY TOO

Enter Love

The love relationships we engage as unrealized grown men are where we usually fuck the pooch most substantially. The reason for this should by now be obvious – soul individuation, the influence of the collective masculine & feminine and the core love/abandonment wound we generated in our own unique ways from our mothers, all operate to create our biggest imbalances by far. The biggest imbalances equate to the biggest consequences, which in turn equate to our primary love relationships being both the place where we express the greatest amount of inverted male power *and* the catalyst for activating our wounding so we express it even more in the outer world beyond the relationship.

There is so much more to heal than almost any of us are aware of. Love does indeed heal all, but what is love… really? Despite the awakening to love I describe here, it would take me another 12 years to fully find that out.

It was actually an attack from the feminine – a drug-induced false accusation of rape, quickly recanted once sober, that gifted me with 10 hours in a jail cell, which I still view to this day as the most significant moment of my life. For it was through this experience that

I was able to discover, for the first time, what kind of man I really was when the chips were truly down… and I liked what I saw. A subsequent vacation to Thailand and union with the goddess who is now my ex-wife then became the catalyst for a profound heart awakening – I felt, for the next year, like my heart was on fire; like I weighed less than a feather – I could see the energy around people; around all living things – I had no explanation for the experience. I suddenly became both every girl's best friend and, for the first time in my life, universally appealing, because for the first time in my life I was not seeking love from outside of myself – I had become love itself.

But this was not to last – a year later and my love returned from her travels, and the care-free woman that I had fallen in love with, was no longer care-free. I was faced with a choice (though I didn't see this so clearly at the time) – to continue to be love, which would have meant doing the self-loving thing and walking away – choosing only to invite experiences into my life that were in alignment with the love I was in this moment, or to pursue a dream based on the 'potential' that it could have in the future. I chose the latter and, like anyone who bases a relationship on potential instead of reality (like we all inevitably do when our actions are under the influence of hidden aspects of ourselves), it would spell the end of my experience of being love itself. For I would then spend all but two of the next eleven years trying to either make her into something that she was not (using inverted male power), or being silently unhappy with her for who she was (the inherent powerlessness which I was unable to address because of my inability to face the reality of my inverted male power). I believed the choice I made at the time was one of love, but actually it was in pursuit of love and the very thing that pushed away love. Any relationship that we enter or maintain on the basis of future potential rather than solely on the reality of what exists in the present is an expression of co-dependency. How many of us do this?

It appeared, on the face of it, that most all the conflict and diversions from love for the entirety of our relationship were initiated by her, and from a 3D perspective that was true, but the real truth was that it was my decision not to do the loving thing at day one, purely resulting from my own love wounds, and my on-going inability to accept this goddess for who she was, that was the real energetic source code of pretty much *all* of the conflict – this was probably one of the greatest bastardizations of the feminine that I have ever committed in my life (that it was driven principally by the desire to see her transcend her own pain rather than to end my own, makes little difference). In reality, she honored me, like I could never honor her and, although she was fundamentally incapable of fulfilling my real needs (as I was hers), she stood by me through thick and thin, never complaining; she loved me in a way that I was unable love her; she followed me to places that no other woman ever would or could – she was devoted, and I will always love her for that.

We had two beautiful daughters together; we did some of the most profound and amazing things together. I do not regret any of that relationship – without its lessons I would never have found my way to my true divine masculine authority and this book would not exist; I would never have discovered my true life mission to remove this false-light scourge from the face of the earth. But it did have the most far-reaching consequences of any breach of natural law that I have ever committed – I am essentially responsible for any negative consequences felt throughout the course of 11 years for two adults, two children, and all those affected by either of us as a result of our relationship.

Life is a series of choices. We make good choices from a space of authentic masculine power, and we make bad choices from a space of either inverted male power, or unseen childhood love-based co-dependent trauma.

There are very few primary love relationships I see between the people around me that do not have a similar undertone – that are not based on neediness; not based on having one's emotional addictions met; not based on fear of aloneness; or not based on a false dream of future potential, etc.. I can personally only imagine the consequential harm caused through the vast majority of primary love relationships where the participants have not had an awakening to pure love beforehand.

Do you accept the goddess(es) in your life completely, just the way they are? Do you maintain your current imperfect relationship because you have hope that it will change... or fear of being alone? Do you want to 'fix' someone? Why are you in your relationship? Did you hear the still small voice of your intuition that said "this one's better left alone" at the outset of the relationship and choose to ignore it? What unhealthy needs do you demand of your partner? What healthy needs do you have that remain unmet that just make you feel unfulfilled?

The pursuit of self-growth

Self-growth is a multi-billion dollar industry, which really reflects just how much a great many of us truly want to be better people. But the question is really whether the majority of self-help programs and tools are truly helpful, or whether they are actually harmful, to one's real evolutionary process? I wouldn't be asking that question if I didn't already know the answer!

You see, the unfortunate truth is that the vast majority (probably at least 99%) of all so-called self-growth programs and tools are encouraging us, without being given proper context as part of a larger picture, to use our false will-power rather than our authentic will. False will-power is that which is driven by fear and serves as the basis of inverted male power, whereas authentic will is driven by love – real untainted pure love that most of us, at the stage we are at when we look to self-growth programs, have yet to experience in an untainted manner.

Busting through our fears, reprogramming our minds/changing our beliefs, and attempting to manipulate the Law of Attraction for our own egoic ends are, in the final analysis of almost all attempts, all examples of the use of false will-power and all a soul depleting abrogation of self-love. There are *many* more, and we have looked at the Law of Attraction already, but let's take a look at these others in more details now.

Reprogramming our minds/changing our beliefs is a technique that has brought relief and great progress to millions of people. So how can it be a bad thing? Well it's not bad; it's just that it is, in most cases, out of harmony with love. Much the same dynamic is at play here as when we also try facing our manly fears, so this lengthy explanation on the dangers of using false will-power to face fears will explain further.

So here's what we men really do when we decide to face our fears when our present base of power is inverted male power; here's what we do when we decide to follow the advice of all those career coaches who have us train our minds in the name of 'self-improvement' when we haven't first properly deconstructing our false selves.

As we have learnt already, when we were young boys and we took the decision to energetically neuter ourselves in order to cease being a threat to the false masculine influences in our environment, we created a sub-personality. We did this by creating a set of faulty belief structures that would allow us to translate our current experiences of life in order that the continuance of those impositions of inverted male power in our reality would be less painful. Essentially we took that part of ourselves that was being emotionally wounded and we hid it away behind that layer of false beliefs – a sub-personality was born; multiple sub-personalities were born.

If we don't take the time to also re-integrate these sub-personalities at the time we make the conscious choice to face our fears, the enhanced sense of personal power that we attain through facing those fears is not built off a base of true divine masculine authority, but rather off a base of inverted male power. Whilst we may have overcome the fear in our daily experience, which may also mean that we experience more love, we have also buried the fractured aspect of ourselves – the pain body of a given sub-personality – deeper. The day will inevitably come where we have to return to collect it, but it will be harder now because the wall of denial we have created around it is denser due to the new false belief that we actually overcame our fears. All we have generally done is face our secondary fears of external things – those fears that are a result of our imbalances – not our core fears that caused us to create the false self that fuelled the creation of the imbalances in the first place.

Facing one's fears is nonetheless crucial to personal evolution – transmuting fear into excitement at the promise of becoming free of fear is a powerful thing – but it needs to be done with gentleness and self-love, otherwise it is simply an act of emotional abuse to ourselves which can only ever add to the problem, and more importantly we need to face the right fear – e.g. the core fear of abandonment rather than the fear of rejection that masks it, or the core fear of facing one's own powerlessness rather than the fear of authority that masks it. The masking fears are simply tools to show us the way to the real fear and the real grief/terror that the real fear is hiding. If we pay genuine attention, they do this by showing us our emotionally addictive behaviors so we can clean them up and make space to experience the truth… more on that later.

Furthermore, it will always be an act of self-abuse to bust through fear using our minds as the driving force if we are facing fears which are the result of the wounding of an unseen fractured aspect of ourselves whose wounding is based on emotional abandonment. We are essentially saying to that aspect of ourselves that "your feeling of emotional abandonment is not valid, stop being a pussy and get on with it" – we're picking up on what was expressed to us as children that caused us to create all this in the first place; we're taking over the role as our own self-abuser.

The wounds that are responsible for generating the fear we experience, be it core fear or masking fear, are emotional wounds. They exist because we suppressed, or were not allowed to express, the emotional pain at the time it occurred. That which was created by the choice not to feel can only be healed by actually feeling it. You can bust through masking fears with the mind and 'action' but you can't bust through core fears in this way – they must be felt, and if we make the choice to bust through our masking fears to experience the false and fleeting relief/enlightenment we may receive, we will be taking ourselves away from the path of real healing, which we will always have to return to in the end. Usually after we've caused a whole load more harm to ourselves and others which we will then need to clean up.

Allow me give you an example from my own life:

So I'm 27 years old, have a slightly dysfunctional relationship, but aside from that I'm happy, successful, have plenty of money – all the cars, houses, holidays I could ever want. I am good at what I do, have awesome friends… everything really, but still I felt disempowered in many areas of life. Sure, I had all these things, but I was unable to avoid my own sense of inner powerlessness – with women; with authorities – with all that really related to the masculine essence… underneath, I was a pussy. So I began to address this; I began facing my fears. I walked away from the world which I had now discovered to be false – the business, the money, the stuff… all of it; I took the decision to be guided by my conscience and by natural law regardless of the outcome – to act only out of love in the external world; to no longer do work that did not serve humanity. I had a major fear of authority. So I began tackling it head on – if I saw an abandoned home owned by the so-called council that had been empty for years, and I saw a homeless person, I would seize the home and house the homeless. I stopped paying the mortgage because I discovered it to be fraudulent (and stopped paying everything else that was likewise fraudulent); I was arrested many times (for various acts of implementing natural law); I brought cases against all kinds of people (judges, police officers, court officers etc.) who themselves were in breach of natural law. I was out to tackle injustice; to right the wrongs of a world gone mad, and I did all of it from a space of love – or at least from the most loving space I was able.

Pretty quickly I was over my fear of authority, and I also then found that things between my father and I automatically shifted – he appeared to be more afraid of me than I was of him.

And so I assumed that was the end of the matter – job done – I could stand up to anyone without fear, I was properly empowered again…. Or was I?

Unfortunately, by suppressing the core fears I had even deeper (for example by addressing the masking fear of authority without looking to the core fear of feeling powerless or by addressing the masking fear of rejection without looking at the core fear of abandonment) I left in place all of the drivers of inverted male power which, because there was a great sense of love and what genuinely felt like true divine power in my experience, would now remain hidden for several years. During those following years, I did a great many things that I would not have otherwise done that had far reaching consequences to others – I created a whole load more stuff, and continued to very subtly express inverted male power in the world. All of which I would ultimately have to address. I also did a *lot* of very awesome, very loving, very beautiful things, but they would have been more awesome, more loving and more beautiful if I had had the courage to face fear truthfully.

After doing all this I discovered several years later that I still had a fear of rejection, but I couldn't feel that fear – there wasn't any in my experience. Because I had pushed through all my fears and jumped straight for the enlightenment, I didn't feel fear anymore, so I removed one of the most helpful signposts for the process of healing. Now I would have to either do it without that signpost, or uncover the signpost first – much harder.

We must be willing to look at *why* we have a fear of something before facing it, rather that beating the shit out of ourselves by running at that fear like a bull in a china shop, because that's just more fear – fear of fear itself. I'll show you how to do that a little later on.

For a man, facing fear is about facing the biggest fear of all – fear of feeling; fear of feeling pain. Facing fear any other way (i.e. by not feeling it) is actually just another act of fear – another act of hiding from our divine masculine authority. And the reality is that fear is nothing more or less than just another e-motion – energy in motion – facing fear, and fear of facing fear, is fear of feeling emotion – we are afraid of an emotion, not of the thing we think we are afraid of. It's enough to make a man feel a bit silly really! So if we want to face fear, all we need to do is be willing to feel energy in motion… not that scary really is it?

'Waking up' and supersizing your karmic debt

One's condition is never static – we are, in each moment, either dying or being reborn, based quite simply on whether the thoughts, words or deeds we are propagating in a given moment are in alignment with natural law or not. The problem with inverted male power is that, at least until we have begun to address it within ourselves or until we have moved through enough of it, it has usually developed within a false self that is in a near permanent state of disharmony with natural law. So until we truly engage our desire and make the full-body choice to align with truth, we are mostly in a state of decline. It is this one thing – alignment with natural law – nothing else; nothing spiritual; nothing esoteric, that is our key to immortality (or mortality/entropy as is usually the case).

But what happens when we begin to wake up to the realities of the world? When we first realize the degree to which we have been lending our energy in to making the world the way it is? When we first realize what we've been doing by playing the commerce game as we have; by paying taxes to fund the war economy; by doing jobs that do little to serve anyone and often actually harm people?

Well, if we have some integrity, we start to find ways to change this – we start to look for ways to realign with natural law. The problem is that if we haven't taken action to address our emotionally wounded selves, we will often take action that, although it may appear to cause less harm to the world and our brothers and sisters, actually makes things worse for them on some level and thus for ourselves (on a soul level). Just like we often try to raise our children differently than our parents raised us, if we don't heal the wounds first, we invariable push back in the other direction and create the opposite (i.e. same) problem). And so it is when we leave the dysfunctional embrace of the male-dominant society.

The point is w need to *begin* with the deep personal work – any other path simply leads to us making things worse for ourselves, and usually also those around us, if we don't. Especially as men, we may be driven by what feels like real love to take action to address the things in our outer reality that are dysfunctional, but unless we have stepped into our true divine authority first, we will inevitably employ aspects of our inverted male power as the vehicle through which to express our loving action in the world... and this is the road to hell that is paved with good intentions.

How many men in this world believe they are truly in service whilst still depleting their own soul condition for not having addressed their inverted male power dynamics fully?

It may be that this is simply unavoidable to a certain degree – when we first wake up to the nature of the world we live in and are compelled to act to change it, we are inevitably very traumatized individuals – we would not have missed the obvious were this not the case. And it's a beautiful awakening – one which we all must go through at some point. Nonetheless with a little more knowledge, maybe we can limit the negative consequences we visit upon ourselves in the broader process of our true evolutionary unfolding?

And let's not tell ourselves that it is ok to do this because we have discovered some karmic clearing technique that will absolve us of our sins – contrary to what the multitude of 'karmic clearers' out there would like you to believe because their business depends on it, one cannot clear their karma without following the process that natural law has provided for us to do so. There are no short-cuts, so be careful what you create for yourself!

The enlightenment trap

At a given point in time on the male awakening journey, a crossroads will come – we will heed the call for the journey to enlightenment, and it is one we will know we must take. But what is enlightenment? Most of us will be drawn by the eastern spirituality version of enlightenment – Firstly, it's the only one widely represented in the world, but secondly, it also resonates most deeply with our 'male' mind-oriented approach to life. But there are consequences for us to this choice…

By 29 years of age, having by then been on a spiritual journey for some six years, I had just come face to face with the truth that spirituality and self-realization/enlightenment have absolutely nothing to do with each other. The inner calling toward the enlightened state had been ringing loud in my soul for many years, but I had been pursuing it through spiritual practice. When I came about the understanding that enlightenment was nothing more or less than the ability to see the world the way it really is; to perceive the truth of all things absent the dirty perceptual filter of our illusory individual selves, that it did not necessarily mean that I was going to live in one permanent mystical state the likes of which I had many times experienced, I dropped pretty much all spiritual practice and focused 100% of my attention on this realization of truth.

It was obvious from the outset what needed to be done – I had to simply make the choice; the choice to value truth above the sum-total of everything else that made up who and what I was – possessions, reputation, identity, relationships… all of it. So that's what I did – I spent endless hours in meditative self-inquiry delving deep into the question of who and what am I, and any other questions of deep intuitive significance – and sure enough, four months later, when my multi-dimensional-self had caught up with that choice, I sat in the garden one day, hopelessly crestfallen at the abject lack of visible progress. I remember saying to myself "well I guess it's ok if this never happens for me" at which point BOOM there it was – I finally saw the truth of life; finding myself laughing uncontrollably at the cosmic joke of just how simple the truth really is!

And so for the next 12-18 months I lived life without there being any real movement of mind; no sense of 'Greg' or separation from anything – it was blissful – and it was during this time that we gave birth to our first daughter.

Now, one would have thought, as was my living experience at the time, that arriving at such a place would be the end of all that other bullshit, and it was, for a time, but the reality was that my false self had not in fact entered into oblivion but had rather simply become transparent – it had ceased to operate for a time, but was still very much there. And it was there for one simple reason – I never reintegrated the fractured aspects of myself before crossing the self-realization Rubicon. And so, in time, 'Greg' returned... the capacity to perceive the truth of life remained, but it would be a good while before I recognized that I was still ignoring vast chunks of the truth of myself and my humanity.

The reality is that this particular version of enlightenment that men throughout the ages have sought to attain – what a very wise man once called dysfunctional enlightenment – is actually a form of denial... denial of self and denial of life. It is escapism, pure and simple.

This particular brand of enlightenment occurs when we 1. Deconstruct the false self by using the mind to challenge and irrationalize beliefs, 2. Face the primal fear of death/non-existence by embracing the apparent nothingness that is hidden in plain sight behind every sight and sound we experience, and 3. Surrender to it to such extent that we realize it is what we are, thereby entering the experience of becoming everything (source consciousness itself embodied). This, however 'enlightening', is a limited state of being.

What we have done, in relation to the real healing process outlined in this book, is to clear all our surface fears and therefore all the negative surface emotion responsible for everything we experience.

What we have not done in relation to the real healing process is clear the real core fear, and thereby open up to the experience of feeling and releasing the emotion (pain/grief) that has been driving our lives. Which means we never really discover our true embodied individuated self, never identify with the truth that we are a soul, and therefore never allow the potential for the fully expansive experience of divine love nor for a true divine union with another here in the physical – these are massive pieces of the potential human experience that we are choosing to cut ourselves off from because of the fear of feeling pain. This is not where we want to be, and yet it is what most men will choose as their path to enlightenment. But it will not last, there is no avoiding oneself.

The true enlightened state occurs when we have integrated/embraced all aspects of ourselves, that is, as a soul based fractal of the Prime Creator (mind), made from and in touch with the earth (body), experiencing the fullness of one's capacity to experience e-motion/energy in motion (soul), yet simultaneously transcendent of it all as source consciousness experiencing itself through a human form.

This is not nearly as hard as it sounds when we follow the correct path and commit to it wholeheartedly… it only seems that way because we don't know what the correct path is. Had I had full knowledge of the correct path from the beginning, what took 12 years could realistically have taken less than one. And the eastern version of enlightenment would not have figured in the equation! The inner calling we have toward the true enlightened state is real, but the eastern version of it is simply male cowardice rebranded. Grow a Pair… do this right!

7 HOW DO YOU EXPRESS YOUR INVERTED MALE POWER DYNAMICS?

Having already an understanding of how the false self is constructed, it is helpful to look a little deeper at what happens when two false selves meet and interact with one another. We already know from the first chapters that in such interactions there is a harvesting of energy – one false self is almost always emotionally/energetically raping the other – rapist and rapee, but let's call them feeder and food for a while!

If we're ever going to master the art of relationship with others – which is the only venue inverted male power propagates through anyway, we need to understand this dynamic – both how it moves in us, how it moves in others *and* how it moves through two people or a group of people in relationship. So let's look at some of the characteristics a little deeper...

Traits & behaviors

Do you relate to any of these traits? Do you recognize any of them in your parents or yourself?

<u>Self-importance</u> – An over-inflated sense of identity often characterized by exaggerating talents or accomplishments, or by

expecting recognition of value without having really earned that recognition.

Entitlement – The belief that either the world owes you something, or that you have a right to receive things.

Superiority – The need to always be right. It can also be more general feeling of superiority which may be characterized by the belief that one can only be understood by special or unique people.

Arrogance – Needs no explanation, but is not to be confused with healthy self-confidence.

Preoccupation with fantasy – Obsessing over inordinate success, unlimited power, astonishing beauty, or a perfect love.

Envy – Being resentful of others or believing others are resentful of you. Envy may more subtly display as the need to compare oneself to others.

Need for admiration – The need for excessive adoration or validation from others.

Or what about these behaviors… do you, or did your parents, express any of these in your lives?

Intimidation – When one is challenged or confronted, or feels they are being undermined, they often engage intimidating behavior to assert their dominance. If there is a specific issue at hand, and once a dominant position has been established, they will then seek to hold the other accountable for the issue by blaming the other for the issue, for which they would otherwise look inferior.

Interrogation – When one is challenged or confronted, or feels they are being undermined, they may alternatively resort to belittling and/or name calling and, if there is a specific issue at hand, immediately blame the other to hold them accountable for the issue.

Exploitation – Where others are seen as objects to be used as needed to achieve one's own ends. When a person has expectations of others, there is almost always subtle exploitative behavior also being conducted.

Accusation & Projection – Where one anticipates challenging or undermining behavior, one may often pre-empt the challenge by getting in there first. They will accuse the other of the things for which they are answerable by projecting their own fears on to the other.

Relentless argumentation – When one is confronted or challenged, to pick a small detail and argue it to the death. If the other person gains any traction in the argument, they will pick another small detail and argue that. Continuing until their opponent is exhausted and frustrated, and the other person concedes the battle.

Abuse of power – When holding the upper hand in a situation, a boss or a disgruntled partner for example, one uses it to

Gas-lighting – The practice of denying one has any accountability for something by re-writing history. Over time the other will begin to question their memory and sanity. The perpetrator now has someone upon whom to easily project and blame all shortcomings.

Diversion – Where one creates an issue out of something extremely insignificant, exaggerating the point to incite the other person and draw their attention away from the real issue for which they would otherwise be held accountable. Diversion drains the energy of others making them more vulnerable ahead of dealing with the real issue.

Fear-mongering – Picking up on another's small fears and elevate them to a state of paranoia. One uses their charisma to weave a believable story with an intense dreadful outcome. Once the other person is frightened, they blame the fear of other for whatever they are seeking to avoid responsibility for.

If you recognized any of these traits and behaviors, you, or your parents, are what we might describe as aggressive expressers of inverted male power. These are all narcissistic traits and behaviors.

***

Maybe you or your parent's inverted male power dynamics are more passive? If so, maybe you will relate to these traits more?

Dependency – A lack of self-worth and identity that creates the tendency to need the approval of others before one is able to feel okay about themselves. Fear of rejection and abandonment makes it hard to leave relationships.

Low self-esteem – Feeling that one is not good enough or comparing yourself to others. Perfectionism and a manufactured false sense of self-esteem are the coping mechanisms one often uses to manage this.

Obsessiveness – Suppressed anxiety and fear that create the tendency to spend a lot of time thinking about other people/relationships, or focusing on one's mistakes.

Poor boundaries – A false sense of responsibility for the feelings and problems of others, and/or an unhealthy need to be validated by/identified through others, which causes one to be emotionally open to others in unhealthy ways. On the other hand, extremely rigid, and equally unhealthy, boundaries may be created as a coping mechanism to close off from others completely.

Inability to be intimate – Shame and weak boundaries create the tendency to be emotionally closed to others for fear of losing oneself or being judged or rejected.

Emotional pain – Hopelessness, despair, anger, resentment and even terror are often triggered as a result of the other related traits.

Emotional numbness – Where emotional pain becomes too great, the coping mechanism is to avoid the pain by closing down one's feelings altogether.

Or what about these accompanying behaviors… do these sound familiar?

Dysfunctional communication – A difficulty expressing one's thoughts, feelings and needs truthfully. Sometimes that might be because one isn't even clear what their own thoughts, feelings and needs are, and other times it might be because one is too afraid to speak what they know to be true for fear of upsetting someone or being attacked as a result. Instead of disagreeing one may try to covertly manipulate the other's opinion resulting in confusing and dishonest communication which only exacerbates the problem.

People-pleasing – An excessive effort to accommodate others and the sacrificing of one's own needs in favor of others. Often it is difficult to say "no" to people.

Reactivity – The taking on of the opinions of others as reflection of oneself which, because one lacks healthy boundaries and are being more open to absorbing the thoughts and feelings of others, creates the feeling of being attacked and needing to defend.

Unhealthy caretaking – The desire to want to help people to the point one gives up themselves, or to incessantly attempt to fix others even when the other clearly isn't interested in being fixed. As a result of lack of personal identity, there may even be feelings of rejection when another doesn't accept the help.

Control – Where one is afraid to take risks or communicate their feelings, it will often result in an over-controlling attitude toward life. Control creates the illusion of safety and security. One may end up violating other people's boundaries in an effort to have control – excessive caretaking and people pleasing may also be the conduit for obtaining that control. Physical addictions may be used to avoid feeling out of control.

If you recognized any of these traits and behaviors, you, or your parents, are what we might describe as having co-dependency related issues. These traits and behaviors are not all examples of inverted male power, but they are the fertile soil in which it seeds.

***

One does not need to meet the clinical definition of a narcissist to have or express one or more narcissistic traits and behaviors, nor does one need to meet the clinical definition of co-dependency to have or express one or more codependent traits and behaviors, nor does one need to have any of the traits to express any of the behaviors. We almost all do express some aspects of both narcissism and codependency a great deal of the time.

8 THE BASIC TOOLS OF TRANSFORMATION

There are four basic qualities we need to develop if we are to be successful with healing our inverted male power dynamics. If we were ever able to embody each of these qualities in their fullest amount, we would already have attained a state of self-mastery. In fact the degree to which we have embodied these qualities is the clearest indicator of where we are at on our journey. So what happens is that the more we go through the process of re-birthing ourselves, the more these qualities grow, and the more these qualities grow, the more we naturally unfold into the process of re-birthing ourselves.

Life is about priorities – if we're going to get the most from life, we need to really ask ourselves what is most important to us. For my part I have one priority that takes precedence over all the others every minute of every day. "By the end of this day I will have grown in love." When you make this your absolute priority, developing these qualities will become a walk in the park.

Commitment to Truth

We need your soul yearning for the truth. If you grow in your capacity to perceive the truth, especially the truth of yourself, you will also grow in self-love, and everything that is ahead will be *much* easier.

Making the ultimate commitment to truth is how we do that. You will never even begin to accept the reality of your own inverted male power dynamics if you don't have a commitment to truth; you will never face the reality of the pain that you carry, or acknowledge your fear of that pain, if you don't have a commitment to truth; you will never face the reality of the pain and suffering you yourself have caused if you don't have a commitment to truth; and you will never develop intimate relationships with others, which requires the capacity for intimate communication, if you don't have a commitment to truth, but all this falls away in an instant once we develop a commitment to truth. No more bullshit. Imagine that.

The rest of this book is either about how to do that, or information to point you to what you need to feel about in order to receive that. And when we do receive it, we think "why on earth didn't I do this sooner?" "how did I ever make life that complicated?" And it's so simple – all you have to do is want it, desire it, value it, share it, above all other things, and you grow in truth.

Additionally, the most important natural laws respond to us according to how much we *want* to know, not how much we *actually* know, so a genuine commitment to the truth, even if our perspective remains cloudy, is all we really need to begin receiving the support of the loving laws of the universe in our life.

Without a commitment to truth we have no chance of ever realigning with the natural loving laws of the universe because our sense of self-preservation will prevent us from seeing the truth of who we are in relation to those laws – we will never even begin to break through the wall of denial, which means we won't even be able to begin the real journey.

Self-love

We need your heart ablaze with love. If you grow in self-love, you will also grow in perception of truth. This process is about re-integrating the fractured aspects of ourselves that we created to compartmentalize our trauma. These fractured sub-personalities are, by definition, the parts of ourselves that have never been loved. They will only return home to us when they release their fear. For this they need love. And the only place they are ever going to get it from is us.

Ironically, the very fact that they exist means that we have been sub-consciously continuing the abuse that caused them to fracture off in the first place. These are all the parts of us that cause us to act in ways which we feel are imperfect, troublesome or childish or which we otherwise loathe as qualities in ourselves. Ceasing to do this and showing true nurturing compassion for these aspects of ourselves is what self-love really is. Loving only the parts of us that we like is the opposite of self-love, it is narcissism.

All we've got to do to leave all that behind is learn to grow in self-love. The rest of this book is either about how to do that, or information on how to develop the right circumstances to feel that. And when we do we think "why on earth didn't I do this sooner?" "what on earth have I been missing out on?" And it's so simple – all you have to do is want it, desire it, value it, share it, above all other things, and you grow in love.

Without self-love we have no chance of ever realigning with natural law because where there is no self-love there is no love, and the universe is all love. The Law of Compensation is our guide – through external reflections – to show us what in our internal state is out of alignment with love.

Willingness to feel anything

We need you open to yourself and get back in your body. If you truly open to *all* emotion, you will discover more truth about yourself, you will develop more faith in both yourself and g-d/the universe, and you will begin to access the parts of yourself that need your love.

If the false self is a self-created entity that we generated in order to avoid feeling pain and avoid feeling terror, it stands to reason that, if we wish to deconstruct the false self, we need to be open to the experience of pain and be able to embrace the fear of the pain. The problem is that it can be difficult (impossible in fact) to do this if we are oblivious to the true nature of our false self — we don't even know what choice we are making. For this we need our commitment to truth to light the way.

Additionally, growth in anything only occurs where there is tension, and tension expresses itself emotionally. If we truly want to evolve then we must be willing to allow that tension and find the enjoyment in it. It is the feeling of insecurity that characterizes this space. Falling in love with the feeling of insecurity is *the* key to rapid evolution. In the beginning this can be a little challenging because that insecurity is very attached to the false self's coping mechanisms, but once we move through this, insecurity simply becomes the sensation of standing on the edge, embracing life without a safety net, in a perpetual state of "yes, please, thank you, more!"

Without a willingness to feel everything, we have no chance of ever realigning with natural law, because the process of forgiveness and repentance, that it the only path that natural law has laid out for us to do so, is entirely feeling based.

Faith

Developing a sense of true faith is crucial to success with this process. We know that making the choice to open to our feelings will generate a great deal of pain — pain which we have hidden from our entire life. We know that committing to the truth above all else will destroy all the illusions that have until now been the only thing we could rely upon to prop ourselves up and get by in life, so they will no longer be there for us to fall back on. We will therefore need a great deal of faith in ourselves and preferably also faith in g-d, the universe or whatever you choose to call it, if we are ever to develop each of these qualities to any significant degree.

Think of faith and truth as bedfellows — there is the truth, and there is the truth that you are aware of. Faith is what you need to be able to work truthfully with the gap between the two — the truth you are *not* aware of. For most people the gap between these two is huge, but as we begin to discover the truth of ourselves and the universe that gap not only shrinks but our faith also grows so we find we have an awful lot to work with.

Without faith we have no chance of ever realigning with the natural loving laws of the universe because we have no tool with which to work to reduce that gap.

***

The key is managing this journey in the most efficient way so that:

- we cause the least continuing depletion of our soul condition;
- we cause the least harm to others through the process;
- we cause the least harm to ourselves through the process;
- we experience the least amount pain possible;

The way to do this is to keep these qualities in balance within ourselves.

By doing this we will naturally undertake each of the exercises we need in the correct order and proportion. So if you have developed 30% of your capacity for commitment to truth, 10% of your capacity for faith, 30% capacity for self-love, and 10% capacity of willingness to feel then, even though you may want to commit more to truth, the most balanced thing you could do is focus instead on developing more faith and willingness to feel. Aside from the fact that this will be the most efficient and painless way to navigate the process, it will also give you a stronger foundation for developing all of the qualities further. As with all things, balance is the key.

It's a choice

If our desire to be loving and caring is greater than our own sense of self-preservation, we *will* commit to growing in love, and the specific choices we must make to lead us to the highest expression of love are the choices to develop each of these four qualities.

To develop a commitment to truth, it is a choice of knowledge and wisdom over self-preservation – true knowledge of self will render all efforts at preserving the false self useless. This means prioritizing the truth over the sum-total of everything else that makes up who and what we are – our possessions, reputation, relationships, identity, etc. Later we look at how to identify where we are subconsciously making the opposite choice so that we can more easily make this choice with every aspect of our multi-dimensional selves.

To develop self-love, it is a choice of love over emotional addiction – to choose in each moment to love in the presence of fear, when our coping mechanisms – control dramas, aggression, victimhood etc. – are running.

To develop a willingness to feel pain is, funnily enough, a choice to be willing to feel pain *and* pleasure. At a given point in life we chose pleasure over pain. Now that we are committed to our own self-mastery there will be a propensity to choose pain at the expense of pleasure because we feel this is what we will need to get us to the 'end'. To do so would be an unloving act towards ourselves and therefore serve only to deplete our capacity for self-love further, because such a choice would be motivated by a desire to end the pain, and that would represent continuing the abuse we have been perpetrating on the fractured aspects of ourselves which have been driving all of the things that keep us from our natural state of self-mastery – it would solidify the problem; it would deplete our soul condition further.

To develop faith, it is a choice of surrendering over resisting and of action over lethargy – to surrender is simply to relax, and true relaxation will help to overcome the blocks and fear that prevent one from taking action. Action is necessary to develop faith because we will never have faith in ourselves if we don't do anything, and we will never have faith in g-d /universe and its laws, if we don't have faith in ourselves.

***

The degree to which we are able to make those choices is the degree to which we desire what we're choosing.

And wanting to desire something is not desiring it. Whenever we find ourselves saying "I want to be more..." [fill in the blank – loving; confident, empowered, etc.], this is not pure desire. Pure desire is an inner longing for something in alignment with love and truth; pure desire is *not* driven by pain. "I want to be more..." is a pursuit of the false self that only exists because the pure desire is absent.

If we don't already have something we think we want, we do not have a strong desire for it, and we need to feel the emotion behind *why* we don't really desire it. The exercise in Chapter 9 – Using your blocks to identify root pain/trauma is an effective way to do this.

9 HOW TO FINALLY FIX IT

Deconstructing the false self is the real name of the game. We know now that this process is a fundamentally emotional one, but by now applying our knowledge of the feeling states we must engage and our knowledge of the nature of the false self, we have a road-map to follow so that we can traverse this terrain in the most efficient, painless way.

Pain is inevitable, but if we do not understand, for example, the difference in our experience between the surface emotions we almost exclusively experience – those that relate to our false self's co-dependencies – and the real core emotions that we need to release, then we can easily find ourselves in a never ending process of feeling pain, because we open up to experiencing pain and choose to stop masking it, but we don't use those surface emotions as the pointer they are designed to be to help us find the real emotional blockages we're really looking for.

So let's take a look at the structure of the false self once again…

The reason why an understanding of the false self is important is because when we know how it was created, we can know how to most efficiently uncreate it. If it was built up layer by layer from the inside out, then the most efficient way to deconstruct it is layer by layer from the outside in!

This doesn't mean that we have to face *all* our denial of everything before we can move on to looking at our co-dependencies, and before we can move on to challenging our false beliefs etc., We can deconstruct one aspect of our false self, and then move on to the next or, as is more naturally the case once we get going, we can be deconstructing multiple aspects at once but be at different stages with each. So, for example, you could be balls deep in feeling the terror of what you experienced at 3 years old when your father was energetically raping you using his own inverted male power, whilst you haven't even moved through the denial of the coping mechanisms you're using which are ultimately hiding your core love wound.

The process

Accepting our unloving behavior

So the first thing we must move through is our outer protective layer of denial… specifically, denial of our coping mechanisms – victimhood, anger, judgment, accusations, control drama's, narcissistic traits etc. – the stuff we have an addiction to expressing. Denial is a tricky customer because from where we stand, the survival of everything, or the vast majority of everything, we experience to be who and what we are, depends on maintaining that denial. For this reason this first step is the hardest of all – to accept all our faults. If we are able to move through it, it is because we have begun to cultivate the basics – commitment to truth, faith, self-love and a willingness to feel – these qualities provide us the strength to venture into the unknown. The rest is just a matter of time and perseverance.

The biggest pitfall, once we begin to look at our denial, is denial of our denial, which invariably plays out as us believing/pretending to ourselves that we are further through the process than we actually are – believing we are at, for example, the stage of looking at our core beliefs or feeling our core fear and pain when in fact we haven't even begun the journey. Being truthful with yourself about where you are actually at is the biggest gift you can give yourself.

All of the natural laws can and should be consciously engaged throughout this process, but this denial stage is where we need to really begin consciously engaging our understanding of the Laws of Attraction and the Law of Compensation to help us recognize the coping mechanisms.

So assuming we have at least begun to cultivate the basics and have a genuine desire to uncover the truth of ourselves, there are a few indicators we can use to see where we are still denying something:

- We find ourselves standing in judgment of ourselves
- We find ourselves making excuses for ourselves
- We find ourselves deflecting responsibility for things – do you really have a right to project your own shortcomings on others?
- We find ourselves expecting things of others – do you really have a right to hold the expectations you do?

Where we see this behavior, or for that matter any of the behaviors identified in Chapter 7, we know that we are denying something. If we see this behavior in response to an accusation or comment of another person, then there are two possibilities – they are right, and what they are accusing us of is true, in which case this is what we are denying, or they are wrong, simply imposing their own denied coping mechanisms on us, and therefore showing us the opposite of what we are. For example, maybe you find yourself defending yourself when accused of not fulfilling your duties at work. If your boss is right, then you are likely denying your sense of entitlement and all coping mechanisms that go with it, whereas if he is wrong, then likely he is projecting his own failures on you in which case you must ask why you are an attraction for such behavior – perhaps you have a tendency for over-giving and so attract people who like to take from you? Either way, by acknowledging the state of defensiveness in you and acknowledging that, whatever your experience, it is showing *you* something about *you*, not the other, you open the door to being able to feel your way through the coping mechanisms and beyond. Just remember – it's always about you, so if you ever find yourself believing or stating that the events of your life are the result of someone else's actions, this is your proof positive that you remain in denial.

An intellectual acceptance of our coping mechanisms is one thing, but an emotional acceptance is quite another – a true intellectual acceptance, absent any justifying behavior is a great step, but we're not going to have sufficient awareness or motivation to stop expressing our harmful addictive behavior toward others until we really *feel* the harm that the behavior is causing. And stopping it is the whole point – firstly, until we do, we are depleting both our own condition and creating more stuff to later clean up every time we express it, but secondly, it is stopping the behavior that is what will show us the way forward. We call them coping mechanisms for a reason – every time we experience a Law of Compensation event, it triggers our co-dependencies, and we feel a negative emotional response. When the charge around that negative emotional response has built sufficiently, we engage a coping mechanism in order to release that charge (usually by deflecting the energy to others). When we emotionally acknowledge our coping mechanisms and the harm they are causing, and we cease using them, that charge will not be released. Our experience of the frustration, anger, powerlessness, etc. of whatever the emotion is will grow. You want this – it will take you straight through to recognizing the false beliefs that are hiding behind it.

This whole process is about you – every time you look at something you look at you, not the other. Any deflection upon the other is escaping from your own truth. Even if you are right about them, so what? Their shit is their shit, yours is yours, and their shit is your gift to show you your shit, nothing more, nothing less. Take the ego out of the equation and this is obvious… all the time.

Co-dependencies

Once we have moved through our denial and accepted the reality of our coping mechanisms, we are able to truthfully look at the co-dependencies we are actually attempting to 'cope' with. It is not actually important to even know what your co-dependencies are in order to progress to the next step, it is enough simply to feel through the emotional effects of the co-dependencies (as discussed above) until you hit upon your false beliefs. If however you are a man like me, then it will likely not only assist you in moving forward if you do, but also satisfy a curiosity that would otherwise bug the hell out of you.

Regardless, we need to allow ourselves to feel the emotions that accompany our coping mechanisms. If we are easily irritated, we need to feel the anger/rage that we are normally suppressing – let it all hang out – never projecting that anger onto others, rather choosing to go to a private space and allowing ourselves to feel it to its full extent. If we feel rejected, we need to allow ourselves to feel the pain of that rejection.

But this is where we must also be careful – because of the tendency most of us have to hate on ourselves for the negative emotions we express and/or the misguided actions we take, we need to really engage this process consciously with love and acceptance. Acceptance is key because judgment, its counterpart, is what is responsible for keeping the anger flame burning.

Judgment of anger, for example, keeps that anger returning because the judgment is a judgment of the fractured aspect of self that is holding the pain that is causing the anger, and that fractured aspect of self is only expressing anger because it continues to receive no love.

To remedy this, the solution is simple – accept all emotion as it arises as pure energy, without judging it as good or bad in any way.

Love the fractured aspect of yourself that is feeling it which, since you can't see it yet, means simply holding a field of love whilst accepting the emotion and allowing it to be felt. This is also a sure fire way to begin to relax that fractured aspect of yourself so that it eventually reveals itself to you more clearly.

Do this, and you'll be facing a wall of false belief in no time!

False beliefs

It is possible that, after moving through the feelings associated with our co-dependencies, we may not in fact hit upon false beliefs but rather a wall of terror. This will be the case where the belief in question relates to a faulty understanding of what love is for which, if we knew the truth, would lead us straight to the core love wound which our hidden self is understandably terrified of. Usually it will be the other way round – beliefs before terror – or there may not be any terror surrounding a given trauma at all, but whatever the case, the name of the game is to feel that terror or challenge the false beliefs.

The only thing one needs to do to move through false beliefs is to scrutinize them in the context of the natural laws. If we understand the laws properly, we will always discover that our false beliefs stand in opposition to one or more of the laws. It's really that simple.

If we are having difficulty comprehending the significance of the laws fully, we can help this challenging of belief along by engaging a process of self-inquiry. Of course we need to know what those beliefs are first, but if we have truly felt through the co-dependency-based emotions that were masking them, then we will know what they are. If not, then we're simply not at this stage yet, and being truthful about this is the best thing we can do for ourselves. If for example you fully felt through the anger you felt when a co-dependency was triggered, you will have found what those beliefs actually are – "I have to earn love" or "I don't deserve love" etc.

Nonetheless, assuming we have identified what those beliefs are, we can now begin to deconstruct them by scrutinizing them in the context of natural law, or using the process of self-inquiry. Self-inquiry consists of getting yourself into a relaxed or meditative state and asking questions of yourself in such a way as to experience the answers – if the answers come in the mind, they are the wrong ones – you want to 'realize' the answer at the soul level, and the soul is feeling based.

The mirror exercise covered later in this chapter is one of many examples of a self-inquiry process. All the exercises throughout this book can be harnessed toward progressing through this deconstruction process. In fact every exercise proposed anywhere in this book *is* part of that deconstruction process. Use everything as your intuition guides.

Wherever you feel stuck anywhere in this process, it is only ever because your false self's desire for self-preservation is greater than your desire for the truth. This is where you need to focus attention – deepening your commitment to truth – when you find yourself unable to move through a given wall.

Fear

The fear of experiencing our grief/terror is the last thing that stands between us and our actual experience of it. We're getting close… but it can also be the most challenging for precisely that reason.

Fear is controlled by the desire to not feel emotion – fear of what will happen if I dare to feel it; fear of being alone; fear of my true self not being good enough; fear of going crazy if I allow myself to feel it.

Facing fear is a case of allowing it into our day to day, moment to moment experience of life – facing fear of aloneness is to accept the obvious reality of your own aloneness and to feel all the emotion that arises; facing fear of not being good enough is to allow yourself to not be good enough and to feel all the emotion that arises.

Although spirits/entities have been influencing large portions of most of our lives for a very long time, it is often when we are open to our fear that their influence can grow. It's good to know this because, as you process through your own fear and begin hearing a lot of fearful thoughts, it is probably the case that many of those thoughts are not your own. Focus on the feeling, ignore the thoughts that arise or, if you can, lean into the thoughts even more – run with the worst case scenarios, go deeper into your fear, use any negative interference to supercharge your own transformation. This is very much a part of the alchemical power we each contain within – to transmute darkness into light.

Releasing the pain

This is actually the easiest part of the whole process – once all the impediments to experiencing pain have gone, i.e. the other stages have been traversed, there is nothing left standing between you and that pain. Experiencing it will just happen on its own provided that you are open to feeling and have developed in the other basic qualities, which you must have done to a great extent in order to have gotten this far anyway.

This is where the Law of Forgiveness kicks in – now at last we know through our direct experience, exactly what we're forgiving the originator of our pain for.

But just because we've now released our core grief and terror does not mean that the job is done…

Reintegration

Reintegrating a soul fragment is the only part of this process which is itself a process, not an event – once we've felt deeply into an emotional wound and have seen and accepted the part of ourselves that was holding it, there may be far less pain but some will remain and there will likely be a period of continuing great sadness. If we skip this part out, or don't recognize when it's time to move on from the grief, we find ourselves trapped in another very male meme – 'suffering for our sins' – the hanged man; the savior.

So once we have experienced the depth of that trauma, it's time to really connect with and love unconditionally the aspect of ourselves that was feeling it. Yes, we need to be ok experiencing its pain and sadness for as long as needed – it won't even begin to subside until you do (if it does it is because you have hidden from it again – i.e. returned to the abuse – not because you have integrated it). And if we are genuine about wanting to accept ourselves the way we are, then we must be ok with the fact that this sadness is a part of it, even if it were to last forever – that's the degree of surrender we must embrace when first processing these emotions. But at the same time, or after a short period of grieving, we need to begin to re-parent these fractured parts of ourselves – this is how they reintegrate. They need to grow up emotionally. They won't just reintegrate because we allow them to feel and release child-like grief. If we don't teach them what it is to be emotionally mature now, they will never grow up and will always be trapped where they are, with you experiencing that suffering forever. That grief is a part of you, and so it will always be there, but when we teach our wounded child selves to grow up emotionally, by nurturing them as we would any other child, it allows for that grief to be transformed into a powerful force which can now enhance our emerging true masculine authority.

These newly discovered fractured aspect of ourselves have the exact same characteristics as any other real child – it has even been carrying a part of your soul essence the entire time.

Consider – if you had emotionally abused your own child for years and then suddenly realized what you had been doing and became unconditionally loving, it is still going to take a while before he/she trusts you fully again – you would have to earn that trust back. The same thing applies here.

Remember – wishing the pain to be over is continuing the abuse, so just allow yourself to experience it. The more you acknowledge and accept all that the fractured aspects of yourself have endured, and the more you love those fractured aspects (even though their qualities are the things you have hated about yourself your whole life) the faster they will integrate with you; the faster your soul fragments will reunite and provide you with a true source of authentic power from which to re-engage life in a clean and self-mastered way.

This process of reintegration is not something that you need to wait to begin either. Your progress through the other stages of the deconstruction process will be greatly accelerated if you begin to address your behavior toward your fractured selves from the outset.

So back to denial – if we begin to acknowledge from the outset, firstly that we even have fractured selves and secondly that we have been mistreating those fractured selves through shaming, blaming, judgment and cruelty toward ourselves, we will begin to soften those fractured pieces and they will become far more open to the rest of the process. Once we have acknowledged our mistreatment, we of course need to stop that mistreatment, but that is pretty easy once we have fully acknowledged it – and I mean to have emotionally acknowledged it so you *know* what it feels like.

Begin to listen to the real needs of your fractured selves and start fulfilling them – take more time to listen and relate to them, allow them to express their feelings, develop more patience toward them/yourself, educate them on the truth that you are now committed to. And as you process through the various layers of the false self, teach your wounded self by example what emotional maturity really is too.

Repentance is a natural component of this part of the process as well – once we've acknowledged what we've been doing to our fractured selves through the years, and especially once we have also begun to allow them to express their feelings, we will begin to naturally repent for that harm caused. It will get easier and easier to fulfill their real needs and allow this reintegration to complete after this point – they will feel understood.

Self-realization

This step is optional, but once we have reintegrated the fractured aspects of ourselves, now is the time when it becomes possible to open up to a fully transcendent enlightened state without causing the problems highlighted in Chapter 6.

There is much information and many teachers who deal with this topic so we'll not go into it in much detail here, but suffice it to say that this can be achieved very easily by reengaging a self inquiry process. But that self inquiry process must now be focused on:

- the question of who or what am I
- facing the fear of oblivion by surrendering to (relaxing into) the apparent nothingness that begins to reveal itself to all who sit and genuinely observe the all-pervading infinite conscious expanse of apparent nothingness that sits behind, throughout and between our sensory experiences. And we

do this until such time as we experience ourselves *as* that infinite conscious expanse which is the source of all things.

***

Once we become more practiced at this deconstruction process, we will find that we don't even need to apply these steps with any real intention. Once we have faced all, or at least most, of that which we are denying, and once we have become attuned to our emotions and developed faith in the universe that we are always safe, we can allow the innate wisdom of our feelings to light the way – they are far more efficient and wise than your intellect at this task. Until then, the logical process described here is useful only to avoid getting lost.

Despite all the 'information' in this book, the objective is not to spend countless hours analyzing the events of your life to make sense of them. That can and should be a part of the process, but *far* more important is your feeling the emotion connected to them so they stop governing your life.

Where we ultimately want to be is in a feeling-led process in which we utilize our intellect for the following purposes only:

- Developing our understanding of natural law.
- Overcoming any fear that we may be experiencing by gaining more knowledge about the thing we are afraid of.
- Self inquiry – for example to challenge beliefs – asking questions of our subconscious selves in such a way that we experience the answer through our feelings.

Likewise, even before we become emotionally adept enough to be fully feeling-led, this does not have to be an entirely linear process. Logic dictates that going through a layered deconstruction phase will be the most efficient path, but follow your own intuition – if and when you feel ready to challenge the core beliefs, do it; if and when you feel raw to the root pain, process it.

The whole process could actually be described as one of

acceptance – complete and total acceptance of oneself in every way. Acceptance of our abuse of ourselves, acceptance of the pain we have been suppressing, acceptance of divine love in our lives, acceptance of the full truth of ourselves. Really it's all about acceptance, and exploring deeper and deeper ways to discover that acceptance, always inquiring – can I accept myself completely just the way I am? What does it even mean to accept myself completely just the way I am? How am I not accepting myself completely just the way I am? Why do I not want to accept myself completely just the way I am?

Feeling

The fact that this is a feeling-led process should be self-evident by now, but it's such an important thing that we really should look at it further.

Our free will is what makes us human, but our feelings are what connect us to our humanity – they are what offer us the potential to be truly powerful creator-beings. Expressing our feelings is how we express our soul. Maybe if you express you feeling fully now, you're afraid it might be a bit messy? You're probably right! A lifetime of emotional suppression has left a lot of festering emotional detritus in our bodies, and releasing that is what will happen when we open to our feelings fully.

But what does it mean to open to our feelings fully? Most people do express themselves emotionally already, and for most it is already messy. This is simply because we are willing to express ourselves in some ways, but not in others… because we aren't even willing to admit that we're hiding from anything.

Emotions being an expression of the soul, if we find ourselves expressing or feeling a lot of negative emotion (well pretty much anything that is not imbued with pure love) it says a lot about the condition of our soul, and is a good wake-up call if we find ourselves deluding ourselves that we are further through this process than we actually are. Emotion is also the only thing that allows us to transcend inter-dimensional boundaries and move into higher-dimensional states of being, so for anyone who is genuinely desirous of conscious evolution, not embracing the fullness of our emotional nature is evolutionary suicide.

Feeling is *not* a means to the end of pain and suffering. Well, actually it is, but it will never fulfill that function until we have also embraced feeling as a complete way of life; until we have made the choice to live our whole life as a *fully* emotionally expressive being. Can you imagine what this would actually look like?

Love is the goal here. We can't think ourselves into love – love is an emotion *and* it is a state of being. Nor can we feel our way to love whilst we are hiding from certain aspects of emotional expression – love is what emerges naturally once we have embraced the fullness of our emotional range – the good, the bad and the terrifying; once we have chosen to be a fully emotional being.

As adults many of us read all kinds of literature, watch all kinds of documentaries, take all kinds of courses & workshops and visit all kinds of healers to try to make sense of and overcome the general unhappiness that exists within us as a result of what we, our parents and society have done to us. But somehow, in the most part, we instinctively avoid books like this that actually lay out the problem and offer a solution, because the problem is too painful to accept and the solution is much more work than one could imagine doing. But here's the thing, there's actually a lot less work involved in this particular choice – the choice to become a fully emotional being – than there is any other we could make, simply because it's the *only* choice that will lead to the desired outcome. Every other choice will lead to more suffering whilst we realize that this was the choice that we really needed to make and then we still have to do the work anyway when we come to that realization. So why not make it easy on ourselves and make the choice now? Pain there certainly will be, but it's far less painful to embrace pain now and move through it than it is to resist pain, undoubtedly experience more of it as a result, and fight tooth and nail until you finally have to concede.

The process of healing would actually take no time at all – our transformation would happen in an instant – if we could just get out of our own way and allow ourselves to experience our natural feelings fully. We won't of course, but that's ok too!

Internal alchemy for personal healing

The heart is a kind of etheric muscle. It keeps itself fit – it stretches itself – by feeling emotion. The problem is that we've all been conditioned to only feel emotion within an acceptable range, so we don't stretch it fully into love and we don't stretch it fully into pain. If we hadn't been conditioned in this way, we'd experience pain as it really is – just another indifferent emotion. Beyond the false beliefs and stories we surround the pain with, that's all there is. Just like the pain in your legs when you've ran too far, or the general muscle pains when you've just been to the gym for the first time in 6 months.

And this is really what alchemy is – employing the heart as a crucible for transmutation. In the case of personal healing that is alchemizing the pain of no love in the fire of pure love, until the pain of no love becomes love itself.

So we then apply this to everything else – transcending the influence of the collective masculine and feminine for example. This occurs when we balance masculine and feminine within. Man is not masculine and woman feminine, we are each both. Balancing masculine and feminine within is a case of feeling the corresponding emotions and integrating them by again allowing them to burn in the crucible of an activated human heart. Feel the shame that the collective masculine carries; the shame of being a man; the sense of being unworthy of the feminine. But feel also the anger of the feminine toward the masculine, which you may initially just experience as a general disdain, which is fine. When we allow ourselves to feel both of these without judging ourselves for being bad men, these feelings will actually become one feeling – the shame and the anger. And we begin to see that the unworthiness is not correct – we feel unworthy of the true love of a woman because of the masculine shame we are so deeply connected to and the collective anger that is emitting from the feminine collective. When we realize that we are both masculine and feminine; that we can balance these energies within us; that we are actually not in fact feeling unworthy of the true love of a woman but rather unworthy of a part of ourselves, then there is no more external projection of our shame onto women – who we previously believed to be the feminine. The shame, the anger, the lack of worthiness, these are all now free to alchemize within us and be transformed into co-creative potential. All of which substantially removes the blocks between ourselves and deep loving intimacy with the opposite sex.

Feeling tips and insights

The willingness to feel insecure, without seeking to move beyond the feeling, is the fertile soil in which divine power may begin to emerge.

The ability to take action that is aligned with your true feelings, and in the face of any insecurities you have, is where divine power expands.

***

Suppressed emotions are trapped at the age at which the suppression occurred. So if you wondering whether the emotion you are feeling relates directly to a core trauma event or not, simply notice how old you feel whilst you're feeling it. If you're feeling into say the terror of emotional abandonment that you know occurred at 3 years old, then you will feel 3 years old. If you don't, you're not feeling the original pain, you're trapped in a cover emotion somewhere. Cover emotions are only there to show you where to go next.

The key to finding suppressed emotion in order to feel it is a case of generating a genuine desire to feel fear. It is the fear of feeling the pain which is the last thing preventing one from doing so, so choosing to feel the fear is how you will be able to find the suppressed emotion.

***

Wherever we are in the deconstruction process, the point is to release emotion, so let it rip – use your head and get creative – it's really simple. Feeling angry? Fucking scream! Wherever you are, without thought, just scream, as loud as you can for as long as you need. And if you feel like withholding from this because you feel uncomfortable, then you've just been shown another coping mechanism to work with!

***

The core emotions we can expect to encounter as we engage the deconstruction process are sadness, grief, fear and terror. But we may also encounter these emotions as we are passing through our coping mechanisms and co-dependencies. This is where confusion often arises. It is very easy, when trying to release core pain, to believe that we are at the stage of releasing pain when we are nowhere near – we mistake the emotional pain which drives our coping mechanisms for the core pain that is responsible for our false beliefs and subsequent co-dependencies. For example perhaps you have a coping mechanism of getting upset when you're your wife doesn't make breakfast for you. Whilst the root pain which gets you wanting her to do this might be the grief that "mummy abandoned me", the cover emotion may also be grief but the story is that "mummy used to do this before she abandoned me, so you don't love me if you don't do it too." They can feel the same but are fundamentally different – the former can't be experienced until the charge around the latter has been released, and the charge around the latter will only be released once the faulty belief which is driving the coping mechanism (and which is actually very easy to identify) i.e. that you are entitled to expect something of another and entitled to get pissed if you don't get what you want, is recognized as false.

Having pain is one thing, using it to justify coping mechanisms which cause a whole load of harm (natural injustice) to yourself and others is quite another.

***

Each core emotion can be differentiated into two types – those which caused us to blame others, and those which made us feel shame or guilt and thus blame ourselves.

When you are blaming someone else, you are not in your core emotion. When you are blaming yourself, you are not in your core emotion.

When blaming ourselves (a reflection of self-loathing), the choice is to feel grief. When blaming others (a cover for entitlement), the choice is to repent for our actions.

You can only have fully repented when you have fully grieved; one follows the other in tandem.

***

As we process all the feelings we have received from the collective and to a great extent from our own trauma, it is normal to be angry at the feminine at some point for being so unbelievably cruel. Who wouldn't be? You were brought into the world and abandoned by your mother, abused over and over by the dark feminine, and generally cast to the wolves. And then it's the feminine that thinks it has a right to hate or distrust men?! That thinks it has the right to treat men as second class citizens? But don't worry, this won't last for too long! Provided you allow yourself to fully feel it of course!

Supportive exercises and tips

Be gentle with yourself

This is perhaps one of the most important tips you can ever take on as a man… the male psyche is conditioned to push, be macho, be strong, and a whole host of other damaging characteristics which, even if we don't display outwardly too much, still cause most of us to be very hard on ourselves.

As we wake up to the false-light world in which we live, the pain of living in this reality only gets greater because we have become conscious of it. There is a natural desire, especially when we really do decide to commit to the path, to want that pain to end – to attain a level of self-mastery that brings us beyond all the suffering. This is natural.

However there are some important considerations here:

1. At a given point in time, the desire for freedom will become the only thing that keeps us from experiencing it, and (most importantly)
2. When we push ourselves through this process out of fear, or out of a desire to see it come to an end (i.e. fear), we actually continue the abuse of self that is responsible for who we are in the first place – we solidify the psychological self rather than diminishing it.

We know already that natural law, in its simplest form, expresses that action based on wisdom and taken from a space of love will create sovereignty/freedom (growth), and that action based on ignorance and taken from a space of fear will create slavery/degradation (decline).

Well the highest form of love is self-love, in fact where there is no self-love there is no love, and since we know that that there are fractured aspects of ourselves that we have not seen, we need to take care to love these parts too.

When we act from a desire to want the suffering to end (fear), we almost always take action which is brutal to the fractured aspects of ourselves that we are yet to see and integrate.

What we are in essence doing if we push ourselves unlovingly along this path is to emotionally abuse the very real beings which are a part of us. Without knowing it we are doing the one thing that we have been doing our entire lives – solidifying the false self by continuing the abuse of our fractured selves. This is actually no different that emotionally abusing your children – in fact it is to continue the emotional abuse that you received as a child which caused you to fracture and hide parts of yourself away in the first place. You initiated that fracturing process so that the abuse could continue against a part of yourself while you could continue through life with less pain.

Please don't continue to do this – act out of love for yourself, which means acting out of love for all aspects of yourself, both seen and unseen. How would you act if it was your own child (which it is) and you saw them suffering? Would you tell them to suck it up and push on through, or would you gather them up and hold them? The latter is the real healing... we've being doing the other our whole lives.

If you find yourself struggling in this regard and if you, like I, have always done your best, then remind yourself that your best really is good enough.

When I was expecting my third child was when I was most deeply engaged with this work for myself and, having gotten a fair way through the process already, was *fully* aware of what was really at stake. I put a lot of pressure on myself to get on with the job. I would find myself wishing I was further along the path than I was or trying to force things along so I would be truly 'ready' for when the child came along. The problem with this of course is that it was continuing the abuse of my own wounded child-self – indirectly telling it that it was not good enough; that I didn't want that part of me. In an effort to be a great father, I was beating on my own wounded child-self. We really do act in some fucked up ways when we allow the illusion of time to influence us!

I, like you, needed to go a little easier on myself... "So, mini me, what do you wanna do today?" "Can I smoke a cigarette please?" "Apart from that?" "Ok, how about a nice movie – can we watch 'Winter's Tale' please?" "Sure thing little guy, I'll go get the chocolate."

Freeing the body 1

Most of us are not even living our lives from within our bodies – we experience ourselves as being a mind with a body. If we were truly in our bodies, we would experience ourselves as being a body with a mind.

Suppressed emotion is stored in the body, so for as long as you're avoiding your emotions it is likely you are also avoiding your body. Your relationship with your body reflects your relationship with the feminine – it is forged from the very earth; our mother earth – if this relationship is dysfunctional, so too will be your relationship with the feminine. Self-love includes love of our own bodies; in fact the relationship with your body is the most crucial aspect of making yourself your own primary relationship partner.

But here's the thing, we can work with our bodies to soften up the emotional blockages it holds by engaging a few simple exercises.

Try this one for yourself, and if you really feel the benefit, you might enjoy delving a little deeper into the topic of bio-energetic therapy:

- Lie on your back on something firm but soft like a yoga mat.
- Bend your knees so that your heels are about 12 inches from your bottom.
- Place the soles of your feet together with your legs spread as wide as they will go.
- Lift your bottom off the floor so that your body is in a straight line through to your knees. This stretches the psoas muscle which connects from the midpoint of your spine to each of your thighs. The Psoas muscle is the central connective muscle in the body – it holds more trapped emotion in the body than any other.
- Hold for a couple of minutes until it gets uncomfortable then return your bottom to the mat.
- Now, keeping the soles of your feet together, lift your knees inwards 5-10cm – wherever you experience the greatest amount of shaking. Hold this position indefinitely.

The goal is to experience the greatest amount of release of bodily tension. You may experience huge amounts of shaking. You want this. You may also experience a large emotional release. You want this too. If emotions do arise for release, allow them to flow, maintaining the position you are in if possible. If you don't experience a direct emotional release, that's ok too – you probably will later!

Freeing the body 2

Sometimes the amount of tension in the body can get in the way of our ability to progress effectively through some of the other steps in our deconstruction process. The purpose of this exercise is to help create the space for a deeper processing of root pain/trauma by alleviating some of that tension. Nonetheless, until the fractured aspects of yourself which are holding that root pain/trauma have been integrated, energetic blocks in the body will keep forming. So if this exercise is helpful to you, you will likely need to return to it regularly right to the end.

To begin, find a comfortable position (sitting or lying down) and observe your body. Move your attention slowly through it systematically, from head to toe, noticing where you may be subconsciously tensing any part of your body.

Pay particular attention to your face – subtle muscle tension in the face that is causing you to unconsciously express outwardly an expression that contradicts the way you actually feel. Tension in the jaw, lips, cheeks, eyes, forehead, etc.

Release the tension, by relaxing these areas as much as possible. Probably the places you find tension will be the places that you have conditioned yourself to store blocked energy in, so you will need to be vigilant for a while as they will want to revert back. Stay with the exercise for as long as possible or until you have arrived at the point where you don't find tension returning to these areas as soon as you withdraw your attention. Continue to notice throughout your day when tension returns to these areas, and relax into it accordingly.

The degree to which you can be present enough to do this throughout the day will reflect the length of time you will need to do this exercise for in order to reset the bodily programming. If you are extremely vigilant, you may find that reset occurs in a very short space of time. Continue to look though for smaller and smaller pockets of tension – the deeper you go, the more you will free your body.

And once you've identified where your problem areas are, you do not need to be scanning through your entire body all the time – simply check in on those areas.

If emotion arises, which is quite likely at some point, simply observe it and allow yourself to experience it without personalizing it (i.e. not attaching your personal/mental story to it).

Using your blocks to identify root pain/trauma

There are other pointers that we can use to identify where a fractured aspect of self is still running the game – where we notice ourselves taking a position on something (particularly something that we feel we want but don't have), like "I really want to connect more deeply with my partner" or "I really wish I had more abundance in my life." Where there is something that we want that we don't have, it is a given that there is an aspect of ourselves that is sat in the background saying "I'm afraid to connect more deeply with my partner" or " I don't deserve to have more abundance in my life," etc.

This is simply the Law of Polarity in action – everything is created dual in the Universe. Opposites are the same in nature, they only differ in degree – and it shows us exactly what we need to do to turn that want, which if not driven by pain may well be in alignment with love and truth, into a reality. To capitalize on this opportunity, we need to discover *why* the part of us that does not want the thing, does not want it. To discover why, we need to communicate with the aspect of our self that does not want it; the aspect that is hiding in the shadows holding the self-sabotaging point of view.

To do this yourself, all you need to do is find a mirror, sit comfortably in front of it – comfortable being the operative word as you're not going to move until you have your answer – and have a conversation… out loud. There are two very real personalities in this conversation – you, the conscious you who feels he 'wants' the thing, and the fractured sub-personality that truly does not. Your reflection is going to be that sub-personality as you go through this exercise. You ask the question "why don't you want to be…" and you sit right there, staring yourself down without flinching, until your mouth opens and an answer comes out. It will get uncomfortable, other emotions, in particular fears, will come up. Be willing to feel them without judgment until they pass. Your face will probably morph in a very reptilian fashion – its presence is showing you that there is an invisible wall between you and the answer you seek. Stay with this for as long as it takes to shift back to normal.

When you get the first answer to the *why* question you asked in the beginning, it will probably lead to more questions. Ask them, find out the answers.

Sometimes however, especially in the beginning, it may be tough to go straight through core beliefs because the fear of experiencing the core pain may be too great – the walls maybe too strong for you to bust through. If this is the case, first release some of the pent up energy around the trauma by simply observing, and allowing yourself to fully feel and experience, as pure energy, anything that arises mentally, emotionally or physically in the body, without personalizing it or looking deeper. Once you have released some of that energy, it may create the space to continue with the exercise, going deeper and experiencing the fractured aspects of self that lie at the root. This more simple exercise is basically dealing with the fear that sits behind the co-dependencies that your false self has developed, rather than the fear at the heart of the matter.

Imagining worst case scenarios for something you are afraid of, or which is occupying your mind, is a great way of triggering a deeper degree of an energetic block in your mental, emotional or physical field.

And imagining best cases scenarios for something which is blocking you, is an excellent way of enhancing your ability to identify the things you need to work with for this exercise. It works because you are 'pushing' yourself to reveal the greatest degree of discomfort around a given block – what about a 'good' scenario are you afraid of?

Throw out the rule-book sometimes

As we reveal and collect up the fractured elements of self, we run in to a wall. This wall is particularly relevant for the fractured aspect of our self that is the one that is harboring the core love wound, and it is this:

The process of reintegration is one of love, but because of the abuse experienced by us which created those fractured pieces of ourselves in the first place, we simply don't have the fully expansive divine love that it needs, flowing in full stream, in order to be able to give that to ourselves. We might have opened to it a lot, and certainly as we continue to walk the path it just continues to open more and more, but it still means that healing is not an instantaneous thing. It means we're going to have to work it through with those fractured selves for as long as it takes.

But maybe we can find some other ways to soften them. After all how can a broken child heal itself with love when it never received any of the kind of love it needs in the first place; how can you perform that healing when you are carrying its core love wound?

When we heal this one fully we *can* be the sole provider of love for the other unhealed aspects of ourselves, in fact that can then happen on its own, but until then we need to think outside of the box…

What if, for just a moment and contrary to every teaching on the subject, it *does* need a perfect love from outside of itself in order to fully heal? What if the stories you tell yourself about needing to provide that love for yourself, when you are singularly incapable, is just more of continuing the abuse? What if you have nothing more to give it than complete and total understanding... even if that feels like you are playing the victim for a while? What if all the ideas and techniques we learn along the path have to be thrown out of the window? What if the only way to transmute the victimhood is to be willing to be the victim? What if the only way to transmute the anger or frustration or powerlessness or sense of injustice is to be willing to be angry or frustrated or powerless?

These words are not intended as a license to be a twat – they are intended to fulfill only a specific purpose – for those who have already found the courage to dig deep enough to fully rediscover the fractured aspects of themselves; in particular those who have already met squarely with that core wounded child-self that carries their core love wound – to cut through the on-going pain that continues when we try to hold to all the ideals that have served us in the past. We're not dealing with an adult any longer – the rules have changed; different needs exist, and maybe, just maybe, we need to turn around and face them in a whole other way?

To determine whether this approach is right for you, i.e. whether you have truly rediscovered this particular core broken aspect of self, you need only look out at the world. If you can look out at the world and witness the child abuse at every turn – the subtle and not so subtle energetic rape that most every child experiences most every day (from the slightest emotional manipulation of a friend toward their child, to YouTube videos ousting serious child abuse and pedophilia) and you are in an abject pit of despair and tears, then this could be right for you. If not, you are either already completely whole and healed, or your own pain is still buried seriously deep and this is not the direction you should be taking.

10 DIGGING DEEPER

Entitlement

Entitlement is a narcissistic quality which informs, directly or indirectly, the vast majority of expressions of our inverted male power, so it gets its own chapter! If we deal directly with any entitlement issues, the rest will be a lot easier to address, and entitlement is one of the easier things to recognize as the false-light in ourselves.

Entitlement is often confused with the state of feeling worthy or deserving of something, but they are two different things. Self-worth is a natural expression of a balanced state – one who knows that they are deserving of all that they desire – it is a precondition of receiving. Entitlement however is an imbalanced state of one who believes they are owed something from the world; from other people. Entitlement is what causes us to take or try to take that thing, be it consciously or subconsciously, from others.

Entitlement implies that one has a right to something, which is very different than deserving something. When we believe, healthily, that we deserve or are worthy of something, we know that we will receive it with grace… and without a fight. When we believe we have a right to something, we often, consciously or unconsciously, take that thing from something or someone. Thus someone who suffers from entitlement imbalances will often not be willing to work for the things they desire – they feel they deserve them without taking action or, for those who are active people, they feel they are entitled to more than their action truly warrants.

Because of this, and given that everything we have comes to us through the labors of people, those who feel entitled will feel that others need to provide whatever it is they feel entitled to for them, regardless of whether they want to or not. Usually they don't, so we either steal it then use our various manipulation tactics to justify our behavior, or use those same manipulation tactics to coerce others into giving it to us in the first place. This is really the same thing as going to your friend's house and taking his car without asking then wondering why he's pissed at you later – it's just more subtle because entitlement, and the manipulation that accompanies it, mostly plays out energetically. Either way, harm is caused and a breach of natural law ensues.

Entitlement does not solely relate to physical things/objects/ possessions either. It is driven by all of our physical, emotional and spiritual needs. In fact it is our imbalanced emotional needs that drive the greatest amount of justified rape by entitlement. The expectation that your wife or girlfriend should act a certain way, or that she should do something for you, is just one expression of entitlement. When we have expectations of others and we react with any of the narcissistic traits/behaviors depicted in Chapter 7, or even if we *only* want to react but don't, entitlement is at large.

Until this entitlement syndrome has been brought under control, it will be impossible for those who suffer with it to engage genuinely meaningful relationships with others and it will be impossible for local communities or society at large to ever function in a harmonious way – the rape culture will continue until mass-adoption, through healing, of the balanced state of genuine self-worth.

Whether you are using entitlement to harm others, or on the receiving end of it, or most likely both in different ways, the path to redemption is the same – attain the balanced state of self-worth.

For the entitled, this is simply a case of recognizing what needs you hold that are causing you to express this entitlement and either fulfilling them on your own or recognizing the falsity of those needs in the first place. Then you must heal the wounds that created them and, if you wish to heal the damaged caused to your soul by engaging the energetic rape caused by your entitlement to date, you will also need to repent for all that you now see you have done.

For the so-called victims of entitlements energetic rape, it is a case of discovering/acknowledging one's deeper needs, being willing to have them fulfilled, and addressing the wounds that are responsible for the lack of self-worth that prevents their genuine and harmless fulfillment by others.

Addressing both sides of your entitlement imbalances is a major step in the whole process which this book speaks to, and it will make it much easier to progress with everything else too.

And, just in case you we're looking to skim past this chapter telling yourself that this doesn't describe you, there's a really simple fool-proof way of detecting whether you're denying ongoing entitlement issues or not – if you feel you deserve something that you don't already have, you have entitlement issues, because if you truly deserved it, you would have it!

When I was dealing with my own entitlement issues I was really forced to accept that, with the exception of a few people, I basically viewed people as commodities. Though I had dealt with much of my entitlement issues many years ago, and therefore no longer 'took' from people to anywhere near the same extent – always consciously aware to make sure that the energetic scale were balanced, the truth was that I still had a major disconnect to people. For the recovering narcissist, this is probably one of the hardest things to overcome. I would be lying if I said I was over it completely – certainly I no longer take from people, energetically or otherwise, but I am still not able to let that many people into my life in a truly meaningful way.

The dark side of shame

We do not need a world full of perfect men; we need a world full of humble men. A humble man is one who is in touch with his feelings; who is willing to feel *everything*; one who does not deflect those feelings by projecting his pain onto others. It is shame that causes us to deflect. Humility – the willingness and ability to feel – is actually the key to transcending every inverted male power dynamic covered in this book.

Shame is at work every time one is stirred into a state of defensiveness. If there was no shame, one could not become defensive. We harbor shame as a result of the blame and fault that has been overtly and covertly thrust upon us throughout our lives, particularly the blame we received as children. Blame is not always overt, so one may carry a great deal of shame without easily remembering the experience of being blamed for things as a child. As a child, blame could have been levied upon us in a number of ways – everything from a subtle and well-hidden sense of annoyance a parent had if you wet the bed or couldn't quite do something right, to out and out emotional deflection of a parent's own shame around a given matter.

The purity of a child will trigger its parent's own wounds, so for example crying, which is a natural expression of emotion, may be met with a defensive feeling from the parent because they feel they are not doing something right. Even though the parent may obviously not accuse a baby of something, their inner defensiveness will be felt by the baby who will automatically perceive that it has done something wrong, simply because the parent is responding negatively to its behavior. Thus shame is something we can begin developing from birth, but worse, if we felt shame from crying we learnt very quickly to start suppressing our emotions, which as we know is the beginning of the end. Worse still is that we are now ashamed of our emotions, so making the choice to open again to our feelings will be twice as hard.

And then of course there are the values of the society into which we were born, which in a great many ways do not reflect the natural laws which we would otherwise naturally express ourselves in alignment with were we naturally nurtured as children. Thus our behavior as young children and adolescents, even when aligned with truth and right action, is condemned by those around us. Our parents were fully socialized too of course, so these kinds of projections begin in the home, but they can ramp up significantly when we venture out in to the 'real world.' If we want to get by in life – experience love, validation, acceptance, etc. – we come to believe that we must adhere to the values and ideals of society. A huge piece of the shame we carry is a result of comparing ourselves to the standards required of us and repeatedly falling short – which everyone will inevitably do if those values and ideals are not themselves in harmony with natural law, which our society clearly is not.

Whilst the vast majority of people have big issues with shame, those of us who were made to feel our bad behavior made us bad people – "you naughty boy" for example – have a rougher ride. Guilt arises when we *do* something bad and is more easily processed. Shame, on the other hand, is a sense of actually *being* bad; it is a challenge to our sense of self which will always be a lot more painful to face.

For this reason, when one finds the courage to face shame, it also takes down a major part of our human ego – allowing us to feel the part of us that falsely believes it is inherently bad will take down a peg or two the part of our self that relies on feeling good and being seen as good by others.

If we've begun to wake up and detach from the false values of society, then great, but what many of us do is continue to run the program of judging ourselves against our own standards. We will almost inevitably apply new standards that are equally unrealistic and likely continue to shame ourselves when we fail to meet them.

In addition to pain and terror, shame is a core emotion – in a certain sense, every expression of inverted male power is a deflection of shame on some level – feel the shame, end the game.

The invisible manipulator dynamic

Everything we have looked at so far in respect of inverted male power very much qualifies as manipulation dynamics, but they are manipulations that can be seen by anyone with knowledge. The particular dynamic we are going to look at here is also a result of false entitlement, but it is much more subtle and difficult to identify, hence why we need to look at it more deeply.

Essentially there are two levels of inverted male power that express through men of good intentions. 1. That which is so obviously wrong based on natural law as viewed from our 3D plane of existence (but which many people don't see in themselves because of their own shadow), and 2. That which appears to be right and just under natural law, and is fully accepted by society, as viewed from our 3D plane of existence, even when we have developed a level of truthfulness with ourselves, but which, from a higher dimensional energetic level, is far from right and just. This more subtle level is what this chapter is all about.

The number of ways in which this subtle dynamic can play out are literally infinite. So I'm going to share here one example of how I was engaging this dynamic on the subtle planes without anyone even noticing.

One principle of natural law is the law of contract – everything in reality has some form of contract/agreement/ understanding as its basis. Without it, life could not exist at any level.

Being an avid proponent of natural law, I have always held these natural principles of contract/agreement as the basis of my interactions. As a result, the three qualities that I have most scorned in human beings are:

- The inability to be true to one's word (breach of contract)
- The making of excuses for oneself (lack of repentance for breach of contract)

- Lack of punctuality (a particularly simple breach of contract that represents a disrespect for people's most valuable commodity – time)

And yet, I was unable to ignore the fact that, with a few notable exceptions, I almost exclusively attracted people for working relationships that possess one or more of these three qualities. Why?

I used to tell myself that it was others who simply weren't capable of a base level of respect for natural law and thus each other, but in light of the insight I was beginning to gain as I myself went through this process of healing I had to look at this again.

What was the common denominator in all these relationships? How did they initiate? What was I not seeing in me that caused this dynamic to play out? Were these people really all how I saw them to be?

The common denominator was 1. Me, and 2. The fact that every agreement/engagement initiated by the other either volunteering themselves for something or agreeing to do something I ask. But in every instance, the reason why they volunteer or agree to something is not clean, and it is *not* solely their wounded selves which are operating but mine too – two wounded selves operating together.

You see, form a purely 3D perspective, my judgment of these situations was 100% correct, but natural law operates multi-dimensionally and so, although I had many years earlier ceased the majority of my expression of inverted male power, I still had a more hidden and as yet undiscovered false sense of entitlement, so what I had actually been doing was subconsciously and energetically coercing people into doing things for me. They were under duress on a higher dimensional plane (a plane which supersedes this one).

Each of these instances arose where a subconscious expression of the others co-dependent need to please came forward in direct response to, and as a perfect match for, my hidden sense of entitlement. I was energetically calling them to action, and they were usually very pleased to do so, even though there was no outward expression in either party of a co-dependent or narcissistic trait.

And what, under natural law, renders a contract/agreement void from the outset? Duress/coercion!

So the reality is that none of these people were in breach of the agreements I thought I had made with them, because, under natural law, the agreements were each void from the outset.

It is entirely possible that each of these people, if engaging in an agreement with someone who was not energetically coercing them into their agreements, would *not* breach those agreements in the first place... this is unlikely to ever happen of course, because a co-dependent imbalance will rarely if ever attract balanced people, but that's not really the point – this was about me and where I have been out of alignment, not them. When you look at mapping your own distorted masculine imbalances, the same will apply.

11 BREAKING THE ONGOING CYCLE WITH OUR CHILDREN

Firstly, let's just be honest with ourselves shall we – the act of having a child without having first healed oneself is an act of rape of innocence in and of itself, because having a child under such circumstances creates an absolute certainty of pain and suffering for the child. In years gone by this was the only choice if we wished to have children at all, but now it is not – now, with the rising awareness we have, it is the first dereliction of duty as a father (or mother). When we own this fully, and repent for it, we truly have the desire to do everything in our power to heal ourselves for our children. It's never too late to be a great father. Nothing we do will ever undo the harm we have already caused, but it's ok – it's what we do in this moment, right now, that counts. The past is history, done. The only wrong action under natural law in this situation is inaction… now. Waiting until tomorrow is the same as never doing.

The beautiful thing about the process described in this book is that, especially if your children are still relatively young, your healing yourself will also heal them of the imbalances they have manifested as a result of your imbalances and, even if they are a little older, will likely be a catalyst for their own rebalancing of themselves.

Until then, the most important thing we can do is to show our emotions, not hide from them – all of them, in front of our children. Leading by example, by feeling everything (yet never projecting anything); embracing everything and loving the part of us that has bottled everything up for our entire lives, is not only how we give permission to our children to do the same, thereby ending their own suppression of emotion, but it is also what our own wounded selves/inner children need. And the fact is that if we can't be fantastic fathers to our own wounded inner children, then we can be damn sure we will never be a fantastic father to anyone else. If society held this one simple value – we don't have children until we've proven out our parenting skills on our own inner child – the world would heal in a single generation.

But what actions can we take with our own children now, as we walk this path?

To our sons

We express the love we think is real, which for boys is whatever they were shown to be love in their early years, often from their mothers and, in respect of how they will later treat women, whatever they were shown the love of a man toward a woman is meant to be by their father (or any male figure) toward their mother. A father who expresses inverted male power toward his wife will program him to do the same to the women he later encounters in his life.

He sees us as God – and there is really no greater responsibility than to be God. So since he sees us this way, we need to live up to it, or he will be disappointed in us one way or another when he realizes we've been bullshitting him… which he will.

Omnipotent, omniscient and omnipresent – how does one become these things? Well to be all powerful is to transcend the inverted male power dynamic and step into one's true masculine authority; to be all knowing is to discover the truth of all things – a natural bi-product of stepping into ones true masculine authority; and to be everywhere is, in the context of a father/son relationship, to be always available emotionally, spiritually, telepathically even when you are not physically present – another natural bi-product of stepping into one's true masculine authority. So basically, by completing the process that this book calls us toward!

The only question you should be asking yourself is "do I love my son enough to face my own shame, or do I love the satiation of pain I experience when I engage my coping mechanisms more?"

To our daughters

We accept the love we think we deserve, which for girls is whatever they were shown to be love in their early years and whatever expectation they have gained from their father. A father who expresses inverted male power, even if only in the presence of his daughter and not directed at her, will program her to look for it in other men. She will attract partners who have qualities the same as your own, so express yourself and relate to her now however you would want her to experience relationship later in life.

They adore us, we are their world – because of our own wounding we have been looking for a love outside of ourselves and never quite hitting the bulls-eye (or never even getting close), and here is a perfect, innocent, beautiful creature who loves us unconditionally – we've got what we've always wanted right in front of us. We've craved an intimate relationship with another human being and now we've got the opportunity to have one with someone who actually wants that with us. And we'd be crazy not to take it, because the kind of man she will be able to attract later in life depends on our ability to engage *clean* intimacy with her *now*. But it must be clean.

If we're not being intimate with our daughters it's because we're afraid. And that fear we hold is the root of all that which is actually damaging her... be it by creating the expectation in her that that is all a man can be – vacant – or by her witnessing or experiencing a thousand tiny acts of emotional rape, or both. So we have a seriously good motivation to look at it all and do whatever it takes to heal ourselves – her happiness depends upon it. We just need to make sure we don't subconsciously manipulate her into fulfilling our own

125

emotional needs in the process. If we are mindful of our own unmet emotional needs and take responsibility for fulfilling them ourselves then we give her what she needs without forming unhealthy co-dependencies.

The only question you should be asking yourself is, do I love my daughter enough to find the courage to face my own fear of intimacy? Or do I love my fear more?

***

If we've made any progress toward clearing our own emotional pain, we quickly arrive at a place where we are seriously fucking angry that they, our parents, did this to us. You will ask why they are not the ones that should be made to feel the pain that you are now terrified of experiencing, that has essentially ruined your life. Well, if you have children of your own and you have been anything other than an immaculate father, you have done the same to them.

And from this space, knowing what it feels like, wouldn't you *want* to be able to experience and release the pain you have caused them, now, so that they never have to experience it for themselves?

Well your own pain is this chance – it is the only chance you have to make good with your own children. It is your golden ticket to repentance for all that you have visited upon them.

12 RELATING TO THE FEMININE NOW

The primary relationship in life must become the relationship with self, and it must be a healthy loving relationship. This is the ground of being which enables us to relate cleanly to the world, and upon which all else relies.

The health of this primary relationship with self will always directly correlate to the degree to which we love ourselves, which in turn will always directly correlate to the degree to which we are able to love others. If you want to have true intimacy with a woman, learn to be truly intimate with yourself and it will happen on its own. If you want to experience the purest love from another, learn to share the purest love with another... which has to be in you first. If you simply want your partner to stop acting like she hates you, find out where you're hating yourself and stop it. This is the simplicity of the path – it's all about you, everything is a reflection of you, so it's completely in your hands.

No matter how you try to look at it, mastering the art of divine union with another is mastering the art of divine union within.

A new relationship template

It is our relationship template that governs each and every relationship we engage, but nowhere is it more influential and far-reaching than in our primary man-woman relationship. This template governs our actions on a subconscious level, determining most every aspect of how we relate to others.

These templates are constructed of information we came here with – hardwired into our DNA, information we absorbed as children – via wounding or observation, and information we absorbed during our pubescent years when our sexual energy began to flow (often erratically).

These relationship templates cause us to variously diminish each and every one of our relationships.

The new relationship template for our species, which we who engage this most sacred of journey's are all participating in anchoring as we clear the collective of its pain, isn't really a template at all – we could call it a non-template relationship template. And it is calling for an entirely new way of relating. A way of relating that embodies the perfection and purity of love of the shared vision we held in the introduction to this book.

The old relationship templates variously cause us to diminish each and every one our relationships by projecting past pain and future desires into the present moment as a result of the false imprinting, stories, needs & beliefs that our false selves have been carrying.

The new non-template, on the other hand, which is yours whenever you choose it, simply requires the opposite – that is, for us to step into a perpetual state of presence – enabling absolution of all that has gone before. We do this by engaging all relationship in the here and now – paying attention to this moment. This always sounds tough I know, but actually it is not something we need to effort towards at all… the falling away of the false imprinting, stories, needs & beliefs we carry, that occurs when we deconstruct our false selves, causes this to happen on its own. Once all the things that keep us from the present moment no longer exist, all we have left is the present moment! This is really the key to a life of presence. Not that there is anything wrong with practicing presence, but until we properly deconstruct our false selves we will always be doing just that – practicing.

So what about the characteristics of the new relationship template generally, for all relationship (when in relationship with those who are also aligned with the new template):

- Empathic people, previously unable to open themselves fully to love for the suffering they experience when doing so, are at last able to do so without reprisal.
- Everyone has become more empathic (as the co-dependent and narcissistic traits that they adopted to hide from the feelings of others are removed).
- The relating itself takes place entirely energetically (as it always has but this time consciously and without any false psychological and emotional overlays).
- There are no containers or definitions for the relationship – the concepts of mother, father, daughter, son, husband, girl-friend, life-partner, colleague, boss, etc. have all fallen away. The essence of the natural familial relationships remains, but there are no more societally accepted characteristics of the 'roles' – everyone can energetically fulfill those roles based on their innate understanding of the present moment needs, and they can fulfill those roles for anyone – as and where the natural impulses of life energetically compel it to be so.
- All that is actually going on, and all you are able to define all relationships as, is people relating with people, in each moment, according to the natural impulses of life (which are now also their own impulses).

For primary relationships this means no more concept of a primary relationship either. What we understand now as a primary relationship is simply another relationship. The primary relationship is of course with self. The primary love of your life is yourself. It is understood by all that we do not really love others (and never really have) but rather we love self, completely, and share the love that flows through us as a result with others. Monogamy, polyamory, hetra/homosexuality, and all other boxes for old primary relationships, no longer exist as concepts, and no longer form part of our lexicon. You will never again call her yours; you will never again be able to limit her in any way; and you will never again be able to impose your needs on her or have expectations of her in any way.

Imagine how many of your unhealthy emotional needs this will challenge! But this is a small price to pay for such a beauty, and although we may perceive from where we are that we will lose ourselves if we do this, all we really lose is pain, and what we gain is monumental. We really have to get this if we are to ever receive the gift of a true man-woman relationship; if we are ever to find the love we yearn for inside.

What if I'm not there yet?

Of course you're not! None of us are ever 'there' – 'there' is the experience of life as a fully-integrated fully-expansive, emotional being; 'there' is the journey, not a destination. When we begin to genuinely desire the kind of relationship we have envisioned together in this book, it will be drawn to us. If we still have a lot of trauma to clear and we're still opening up to our emotional selves fully, then the other whom we attract will be someone who has corresponding traumas who also wants to work through them consciously. This is really the most amazing thing – to engage the healing process *with* a goddess, in mutuality, painful as it may be at times, is a tremendously beautiful thing. I am very glad I didn't wait until I was 'clean' before I attracted this kind of a relationship, I would have missed out on so much – the trust that is built as you develop a level of intimacy through sharing everything there is to share; the trust that is built as you trigger, challenge and intentionally move through everything that you each have suppressed within you, never straying, always there for each other no matter what; the remarkable gift of sharing the full experience with another of the completion of the greatest work life has to offer… beautiful.

Two things must be present to traverse such territory with another – 1. a deep soul connection (which we easily attract when we are genuinely desiring it), and 2. a commitment. But it is a commitment – mind, body and soul – to the energy of pure love that you share as a result of your connection, *not* a commitment to the person. When two people are doing this, and they are naturally compatible, an unshakeable bond will form between them unlike any other. It is the only way in which true loyalty can emerge. When we are committed to the energy rather than the person, we can allow the entirely natural flow of wanting and not wanting, that is a natural part of every man-woman relationship, to run its course. The biggest mistake we make in primary relationships, which we make only because of our unconscious emotional wounds, is to attach ourselves to the wanting – we don't allow for the natural ebb and flow of the energy between us and instead cling on to it when we feel it waning. We interpret a waning in the flow of energy between ourselves and the other as a loss, when in fact it is not only natural, but a gift that helps us maintain our individuality. Clinging to it is the only thing that prevents that natural desire from returning in its own natural flow.

You can't beat nature, so you may as well join it… this means living in alignment with the loving laws of nature and allowing things to flow naturally beyond any and all ideas of what we 'think' something should be.

***

We will never step into the fullness of our true divine masculine potential until we can engage a true man-woman relationship. And we will never be able to engage a true man-woman relationship until 1. The aspects of ourselves that experience the felt but unseen divide between the sexes have gone, and 2. The aspects of our partner that likewise experience that divide have also gone.

The first aspect of this will, in part, be a natural bi-product of engaging the lifestyle and process outlined in this book, but the second aspect of this will not. And in any event it will never be possible to fully heal the masculine/feminine divide, even in you, without engaging true man-woman relationships. That doesn't mean you have to be perfect, but it does mean a steadfast commitment to striving for the kind of true man-woman relationship described in this chapter, and it does mean only engaging intimate relationships with the opposite sex where they have an equal desire and motivation to experience the same kind of relationship. Any other kind of relationship is really only serving to deplete your condition further.

Everything else that follows needs to be built off these foundations, otherwise your attempts to implement what follows will be futile – when you have embodied a certain degree of self-love, you simply won't be willing to be in a man-woman relationship where these conditions aren't present anyway, but choosing this now will make it a much easier ride.

If you do base your man-woman relationships off this principle then they *will* become your greatest gift to propel you at lightning speed along your own journey to self-mastery. And if you do have this foundation, then really there are only three things you need to do to begin – 1. Overcome your distrust of the feminine, 2. Develop open communications, and 3. Commit yourself to honoring the goddess(es) in your life completely… in no particular order.

Overcoming distrust

Distrust of the feminine supercharges our core love wound. And you have a lot of reasons not to trust the feminine. It has brutalized and wounded you just as you have brutalized and wounded it. This distrust is two-sided, but we will never break through it if we do not find some real courage. Courage, by definition, is to proceed in the presence of fear, and make no mistake – we are afraid. Just finding the courage to simply own this fear and accept it is real is the first step.

For me this distrust subsided in stages – first when I experienced an other life experience that matched my own state, next when I finally released the terror and grief surrounding my core love wound, and finally when I had the unexpected experience of returning to the original moment of first incarnation, when my unified soul divided into masculine and feminine counterparts – my soul's first ever experience in a self-aware state was to experience the feminine as other and the sense of loss of the unified state. Going right back to feeling the original sense of loss that began at the point of first incarnation brought by far the greatest release of feminine distrust, because although this event may not in itself have created distrust, it was the biggest aggravator of the later traumatic events in my life that did.

Communication

Communication is the foundation of all relationship, but in no other situation is it as significant as in a true man-woman relationship. A true man-woman relationship between two people who are not already in a state of self-mastery as individuals, is one that is purposed *solely* toward becoming such, and the reason why such relationships are the key to personal transformation is because they are where we can find our most painful reflections.

So the commitments we make to each other are five-fold:

1. To speak the truth of our own feelings – we must be willing to face our fear of being vulnerable; our fear of being seen fully for what we are; our fear of rejection; our fear of everything – we must *want* to speak the *full* truth of ourselves and what we feel, more than we want to maintain our fears and false sense of identity.
2. To listen without reacting to the truth the other expresses about their feelings – we must *want* to hear the full truth of the other, no matter how much pain it creates for us. And

we must choose to prioritize their needs over our own need to preserve our false sense of self, by not reacting to what they have to say when we are inevitably triggered by what the truth of their feelings reveals. The truth of the other's feelings will very often cause us a great deal of pain, but if we are committed to this path, we *want* those painful reflections because we know that they will propel us to heal whatever trauma is responsible for the pain in the reflection. And believe me, it is a gift of unparalleled proportion to have the kind of relationship where we can get those reflections without actually being in the 'danger' situations where we normally otherwise receive them.

3. To only speak about something which relates to the other in terms of how it makes/has made us feel, *never* using accusatory language or any language that would be received as being an attack. "When you did X, it made me feel Y…" not "When you did X, you did Y to me…"

4. To share *everything* about how we feel, no matter what it is, irrespective of the fact that we are afraid it may hurt the other – if we have honored commitment 3 when we speak it, nothing we say can ever harm the other, only their own trauma is capable of triggering the feeling of hurt. If we truly love the other, we would not deny them the truth that could lead to their healing themselves, we would only deliver that truth in the most loving way. This has nothing to do with expressing what we think/feel about the other's healing process – that is theirs to do, yours is yours. Advice should only be offered when requested.

5. To make no other commitments until we are through with our mutual healing!

You will find, when two people each truly engage this very simple format of communication, that it will build a level of trust and intimacy that is nothing short of biblical; it will provide the foundation for everything else that you could ever imagine a true man-woman relationship to be.

Such open communication will ultimately lead to a telepathic connection and, if you can each arrive to the point at which you both re-connect with your core wounded child-self, and both dwell in that space together, allowing each other to connect with each other's wounded child-self, it will be the first time in your life that you will ever have known someone completely, and thus the first time you have ever had the opportunity to love someone completely just the way they are. It will also be the first time anyone else will ever have known you completely, and thus the first time it will ever have become possible for you to be loved completely by another. And when this happens, something else beautiful will also happen – every personal need, want or desire in you will be wholly drowned out by the compulsion to protect; to protect innocence and pure love itself. This is about the biggest boost we can ever receive toward our effort at transcending our inverted male power dynamics.

Honoring the goddess

So being that we're walking the path but aren't fully there yet, our capacity to honor the goddesses in our lives is only equal to where we are at now. We oughtn't chastise ourselves for not being able to honor her fully – rather we use our inability to do so as the motivational force to do whatever it takes to be able to do so.

If this is a game you are willing to play (and you'd be crazy not to as it is the most beautiful aspect that the game of life has to offer), there are a few golden rules which, if you follow, will have her beginning to open up to you completely and have both of you facing your shadows and climbing the ladder to self-mastery faster than shit off a hot shovel.

Everything shared in the remainder of this chapter are simply pointers – a few insights from one whose life is all about evolving in love to perform the sacred task of honoring the goddess. In reality we each must step into our own perfect version of divine masculine embodiment which means we really have to figure this out by ourselves as we go – the goddess needs the divine masculine, and a man may only become such by believing in himself… or perhaps more accurately by not not believing in himself!

Some golden rules

1. Communication is the key to everything. The more we share the intimate details of our feelings, the more she will share hers, and the faster both will be propelled toward their own perfection.
2. They are already and always all goddesses – if you really look closely, she always has been. When we notice that we're perceiving otherwise, it's just another beautiful Law of Attraction that is showing us what we need to do next.
3. They are our greatest teachers… always. We can't pull the goddess out of her shell. We can't force her into bloom. The only way we can support the goddess rising is to allow her to teach us, and in our allowing her to teach us – from wherever she is right now and wherever we are right now – we are giving her the support to step out further. The same is true in reverse for this and most of the other rules, but we can't impose that, or expect it – that's just more false-light entitlement.
4. Every goddess needs just one thing in order to step into her full potential, that is – to feel seen, supported, safe and loved. Find the strength to give her this, without *any* of your own needs being mixed in with it, and she will blossom faster than you ever thought possible.
5. She can never be our property, no matter how much we try to make her so. She may only ever be 'your' goddess when you have set her free… in every way… and even then maybe not, but it won't matter by then anyway!
6. Adoring or worshiping the goddess is the opposite of honoring the goddess… she is not 'better' than us, nor is she

less than us, she is simply a perfect divine creation of love itself, just like we are. Honoring ourselves is the key to honoring the goddess.

7. 'I want' has no place in any way with our relationship with any goddess – transcending our own needs where we can (i.e. where they are false needs of the false self – which, I'm sorry to say, is all of them!), and fulfilling them ourselves where we can't, is the only way to go.

8. 'You are doing X to me' has no place in any way with our relationship with any goddess – we must stand in our own power and allow her to be whatever she needs to be, or get out of her way if we can't.

9. If we are not living in awe at how lucky we are to be graced with the presence of a goddess for just this moment alone, we haven't yet discovered what honoring the goddess *really* means – find the awe.

10. If you used to see the goddess in her when you first entered a relationship and you don't so much anymore, sort *your* head out – it is you that has changed not her... regardless of what your false self may be telling you.

11. She deserves only love... all of the time. Our job is simply to be that.

These next guidelines are more about love making – sexual energy is the basis of all creation, so dealing with our sexual issues is a huge piece of experiencing a true man-woman relationship in all areas of life:

12. Our sexual neediness is our own worst enemy. Deal with this as a priority.

13. Let her lead. That doesn't mean be submissive (though it might if that's what she is calling for), it means attune yourself to her energy and follow it – if she is screaming on the inside to be taken, take her; if she is radiating the energy

of a wild lioness then let her attack – follow the energy moment to moment. This actually goes for everything you engage with her, not just love making.

14. If she falls out of the space of natural flowing loving intimacy while you are in the act of love making, don't push – allow her to lead. Stay where you are, pick up on how she feels, hold her, it might be five minutes, or it might be two hours until she steps back into that energy, or it may be not at all. If you're going to honor her, you need to not only accept this, but love her for it. If she doesn't feel any sense of obligation resulting from your own projections, she will open to you much more in every area of life.

15. If you are the one to fall out of the space of natural flowing loving intimacy, so will she. If that happens, go as easy on yourself as you would do with her.

16. Anything that your false self is still 'wanting' will *only* come if you allow the space for it not to come – perhaps you're having an intimate moment and want to make it more physical? Let go of that. Take that false-light desire and process it – just as we discussed earlier. Let her lead, enjoy where she takes you, and you will have far more fun than if you got your own way anyway.

17. Feel gratitude that she is willing to be patient with you whilst you do all this… even if she isn't!

18. Love yourself every bit as much as you love her, in fact if you don't, you won't be able to love her at all. Self-love doesn't mean what we think it means – it means loving *all* of ourselves, but most particularly those parts that we don't even know exist and which we have been brow-beating since the moment we hid from them.

Getting over sexual neediness

Most men suffer from some form of sexual neediness. There are very simple reasons why this happens – sex is a primal drive for both men and women. On a primal level we do 'need' sex. But the problem of sexual neediness has nothing to do with this primal drive, and everything to do with the co-dependencies existing in our false selves. The primal sex drive may be the fuel for those co-dependencies to express sexual neediness, but it is not responsible for it.

Getting over our own sexual neediness is actually very simple, it can be a little painful too, but only if we let our false selves get involved too heavily in the process!

First of all, we need to get real with ourselves – if we don't already feel like a sexual legend, we're almost certainly holding some kind of sexual neediness – own it.

Look at it deeply – we don't need all the intellectual details, we just need to *feel* it – how does it feel to be like a spoilt little child? Ask yourself the tough questions – it is in your best interest to exorcise this shit swiftly (never go so far as to abrogate self-love though).

It is good to allow the clearing process to reveal itself to you rather than being attached to any specific path laid out here. Just feeling it should be enough to show you what to do next. i.e. to show you what to process using the other techniques shared in this book to lead you out of the neediness.

But there's much more to the sexual aspects of stepping into one's true masculine potential than simply transcending sexual neediness.

Fuck something else instead

We must never try to deny the aspect of ourselves that feels the need to fuck just because we have stepped onto some spiritual path which is telling us to honor the goddess. Honor the goddess absolutely, in every imaginable way you can find, but if you try to deny the truth of who and what you are in this moment, or what your real needs are, it will *not* lead you to the outcome of fulfilled man-woman relationships, it will make you impotent.

But should we be fucking our goddesses? Well, maybe, with pure love, yeah, if that's what they want, but chances are, until we've really mastered ourselves, that is not what they really want from us… at least not as often as we might want it anyway (and even if they do, it does not discount what follows).

So what to do? Start fucking something else – something that was designed to be fucked; something that has had its legs spread wide since the day you were born, begging to be fucked... and learn how to fuck it with love. We're talking here about *life*...

When we lead lives that are not the highest expression of ourselves, we find that we are living (a half) life and fucking women (with little real love).

When we step into our authentic masculine essence and live the highest expression of ourselves, we find that we are fucking life (with all love) and truly loving women.

In essence, this is really the only way to honor the goddess, because a man who is not grabbing life by the pig-tails, has little more to offer the goddess(es) he chooses to love anyway than emasculated love... which is not what she needs.

So what does it take to step into your true masculine authority as a fully-embodied, bona fide fucker of life? It takes becoming love; it takes being able to really feel; it takes the ability to live a manifest life of purpose; and it takes the absence of fear, all of which are, funnily enough, natural consequences of deconstructing our false selves!

What more can I do?

This lovely little practice came to me from a good friend of mine who has been truly honoring the goddess for over 50 years. It is incredibly simple, but will keep your focus on the task at hand and help you get very creative at finding new ways to honor the goddess.

At the end of *every* day, when you are lying in bed, review your day and ask yourself this question – what one more thing could I have done today to have made her life easier or better? Tomorrow, if it's still relevant, do it.

The ultimate opportunity

There really is no better, faster, more efficient way to traverse the path to our own self-mastery than to have the starkest reflection of ourselves, mirrored through the goddess, to show us everything about ourselves that is not truly liberated. Of course the faster we travel the path, the more pain we will experience in a shorter time – everyone has to pay the Man his full dues, but I for one just wanted all that shit out of me as quick as possible, regardless of what it took. If you feel the same, the goddess is your key.

It is our sacred duty as men, to be all that we can be – for ourselves, for humanity, for creation, but most of all for our women. They too must become whole, but we made them un-whole so it is we who have the response-ability to turn the tables, anchoring the divine masculine /feminine within as an energetic beacon to raise the goddess out of its man-imposed prison. The goddess is doing this on its own of course, but we will never meet her there unless and until we are willing to take full response-ability too.

So time to get your ass out there and love the goddesses – all of them – completely, cleanly, intimately, expansively, no holding back!

THE END

I do hope you enjoyed this book. If you did, please don't forget to leave a review on Amazon – that's how the information shared here can reach even more people. Thank you

EPILOGUE

A shift is happening right now on earth – we see the symptoms of this shift playing out in the world; in the media; everywhere we turn. Many will probably think they know what I'm referring to here, but I'm not referring to the so-called shift in consciousness that the alternative media is all over, I'm talking about the core essence of that shift – what's really driving it.

The first real symptoms that revealed in mainstream awareness of this driving force were the media focus on child abuse, pedophilia, even domestic violence in general, and how the reaction of people to these stories began to become more emotive than ever. This was followed by concerted attempts to actually do something about it for the first time, but why?

Put simply, it is the arising desire to protect innocence – this is the major shift that is happening on the planet today. To its fullest and purest extent, it has occurred to but a few people, but subtly, in the hearts of billions, it is beginning to arise – like a brewing volcano it is smoldering, rising steadily, and poised to explode.

It is arising in us because, on some collective unconscious level, we are being called to evolve, and to evolve we must heal. And at the heart of every wound of every human being alive on this planet who is not living an enlightened life, lies a wound so raw that it remains unspeakable to all but a few – the wound that lies at the heart of our broken self that fractured itself off and hid away behind the most insidious of belief structures; it is the part of each of us that had our innocence robbed; it is the part of each of us that experiences so many of the interactions we have in the world as the rape that they are… even though most barely perceive it. That wound is masking the inherent innocence which is the essence of who and what we are, and the scab is beginning to fall off… for us all.

As and when we find the courage to lean in to this shift which is occurring within us, as you who are reading this book must now be ready to do, we eventually come face to face with this innocence in ourselves, and then we begin to see that innocence in everyone and everything around us – the desire to protect it supersedes every other desire we have, and it renders impotent every emotional addiction we've hitherto used to justify our own destruction of innocence. As this phenomenon continues to plays out, it will change the world. It is at last the blossoming of a seed – planted at the beginning of time – that has held sacred the promise of true peace, true freedom and true liberation on earth.

A storm is coming people, and when it has passed, it will be, for the first time, the innocent who are left standing.

Let us allow the authentic masculine power in us to fight for that – by loving it, and becoming it.

Aho

ABOUT THE AUTHOR

Greg Paul left behind a successful career as a construction professional and business owner, following a deep awakening to the nature of himself and reality, to take a deep dive into an authentic sovereignty adventure that continues to this day.

Greg holds that sovereignty – true sovereignty – is so much more than freedom from governmental oversight, it is freedom from everything and everyone including, most significantly, freedom from oneself, and is fiercely dedicated to supporting all those who are ready to do all that it takes to exit stage left from the mutant reality matrix to re-birth oneself – body, mind and spirit – into a heaven which is already here. In 2016 he founded an online learning community – The Sovereign's Way Academy – where he shares his insight and knowledge to support this objective.

To Greg it is not just about stepping into our authentic sovereign power, but harnessing that power and the true creative potential it carries to manifest patterns of perfection in the outer world. He lives this example, having also co-created multiple 'externalized' projects and initiatives that support this internal sovereign awakening by offering an alternative to the planet-wide slave system which has too long plagued mankind. He is one of the principal masterminds behind New Earth Project/New Earth Nation which is, amongst many other things, leading the charge on the proliferation of free energy and other advanced technology; developing community and other projects; and engaging with free-thinking governments to create extensive developmental global exemplars of conscious, sovereign community-in-action. He is also one of the original creators of the International Tribunal for Natural Justice – the world's only court of natural justice mandated by real men and women to tackle issues and injustices of global consequence.

Made in the USA
Coppell, TX
23 January 2020